This Book Belongs to

Find Us On

Website www.adropfromeden.com

Instagram https://www.instagram.com/adropfromeden/

Twitter https://twitter.com/adropfromeden

Facebook aromatherapy group https://www.facebook.com/groups/
adropfromeden

Facebook Ministry Group https://www.facebook.com/groups/
adropfromedenministry

About The Author

Hello Everyone, my name is Felicia Patterson. I am an author, and minister, have a master's in aromatherapy and skincare, and am a psychology major. I was born with a rare spinal and immune deficiency that made physically going to school impossible. For this reason, I was hospital homebound from birth. My parents homeschooled me until I surpassed them, then did a combination of virtual education and having teachers sent to my home. This experience inspired me to create content that both helps achieve common core standards while making learning fun. Being the youngest of six whom did brick and mortar education. I fully believe that being home-taught not only gave me a much better education, the ability to achieve things faster, to be self-disciplined, and a free thinker, but also a life perspective that most don't have.

Make Learning Fun

5 FRIENDS

There were **5** friends one was paralyzed he could not walk.

4 friends took their friend and carried him to where they heard Jesus talked.

The place was crowded they couldn't get in.

They said, "To the roof we will carry our friend!"

So up they climbed friend and all.

They threw off the tiles and the straw

They lowered their friend into the hall. They lowered the man bed and all.

When Jesus saw the **5** friends faith, He declared, "Your sins are forgiven, be healed and walk."

The paralyzed man jumped to his feet,
and picked up his bed just like Jesus said.

The **5** friends rejoiced and went their way, never to forget how Jesus healed their friend that day.

Story is from Luke 5:17-26

This story shows it's our faith in Jesus that brings salvation and healing.

Jesus was telling all who were there that day that as He could forgive sins He healed the same way.

We need only believe and live by faith knowing that Jesus is the same for us as in that day.

SO JUST BELIEVE AND DO NOT DOUBT JESUS' WORD WILL WORK IT OUT!

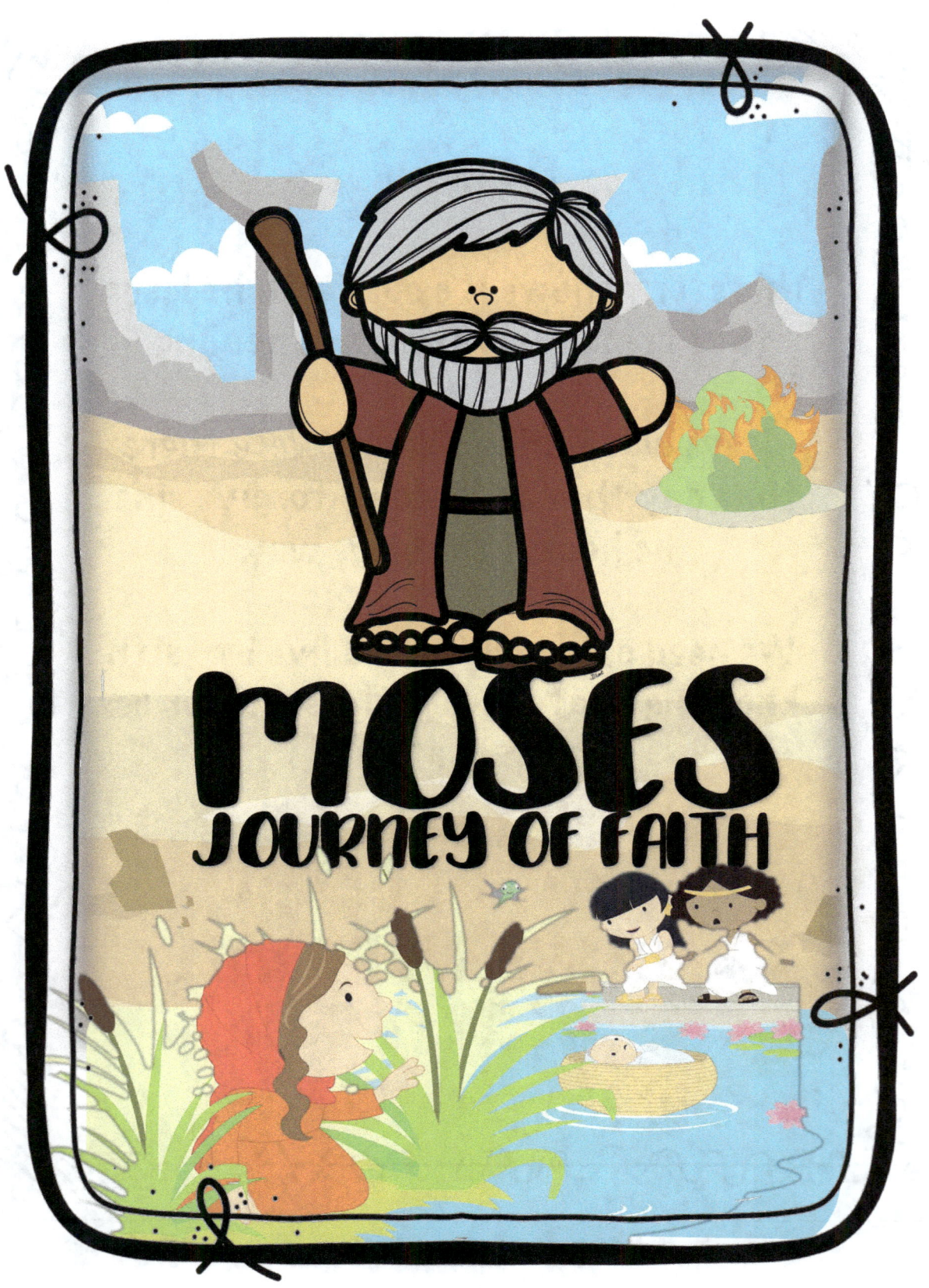

Women of Courage

Faith and courage is interwoven into Moses' life, even prior to his being born. His lineage was from Abraham, Isaac, and Jacob men of faith, in fact Abraham is called our father of faith when we become born again receiving Jesus and all He has done for us.

The king at this time is full of fear and pride. He tells his people, "These Israelites are dangerous to us because there are so many of them. Let's figure out a way to put an end to these Israelites. If we don't should war break out, they will join our enemies and fight against us and escape out of our country.

FEAR – ALWAYS TELLS YOU THE WORST ABOUT OTHERS AND SITUATIONS.

What did he do? He made slaves of them and treated them harshly. But the more this king and the Egyptians mistreated them the more they multiplied.

This is God's way, when His people are mistreated and oppressed, He causes them to increase not only in His blessing but in numbers.

The king decides he's going to kill every baby boy that is born. Who is this king listening to? _____

This king is listening to Satan and fear, so he tells the 2 midwives Shiphrah and Puah to kill the babies before they are born. These two-woman feared God more than the king.

Put this verse in your heart! Jesus said,

♡ ♡ ♡

"FOR WHOEVER DESIRES TO SAVE HIS LIVE WILL LOSE IT, BUT WHOEVER LOSSES HIS LIFE FOR MY SAKE WILL FIND IT."
MATTHEW 16:25

Is it easy? **no**

God will always cause you to TRIUMPH! This always causes alarm in God's enemies.

HEROINES OF FAITH

SHIPHRAH AND PUAH

Women of Courage

These two-woman Shiphrah and Puah because they refused to kill the baby boys their story and courage was spread throughout the Israelites.

Now the king says, once these babies are born if it is a boy kill it, but a girl can live. How abominable this king is to kill newborn babies all because he is afraid.

A woman of the Hebrews has a baby boy, and this woman is a woman of faith and courage. She hides her baby for 3 months. When she no longer can hide her baby she weaves together a stray basket, and seals it with mud and straw and then she puts her baby in the basket and puts it into the river. She instructs her older daughter to watch and follow the basket to see where it goes.

This woman did everything she could do to save her child, putting him into that basket and into water she is trusting God to do His part.

God never fails. God always acts when He sees faith.
Perfect timing, Pharoah's (the kings) daughter comes to the river to bath, and she sees the basket and tells her maids to go bring the basket. She looks inside and she finds a precious baby boy crying.

The sister of this baby boy was also a young girl of courage she speaks up. Because she does Moses is brought back home to be taken care of by his own mommy. Even more than that this mommy gets paid to take care of her own baby boy Moses.

Put this verse in your heart!

"NOW TO HIM WHO IS ABLE TO DO THE EXCEEDINGLY ABUNDANTLY ABOVE ALL THAT WE ASK OR THINK, ACCORDING TO THE POWER THAT WORKS IN US."
EPHESIANS 3:,

WHAT IS THAT POWER THAT IS WORKING IN YOU?

FAITH and COURAGE

GOD'S PLAN

God has a plan for each and everyone of us for our life. It's a great plan. It's a plan to bring us good and not evil. It's a plan that we will love and enjoy.

BUT...we can get off the plan God has for us.

Moses knew he was a Hebrew. Moses grew up in the Pharoah's palace with all the comforts and riches this provided. But he didn't want to be considered an Egyptian. He loved his lineage as a Hebrew.

He has grown and now he goes throughout Egypt and sees the Hebrews working and being mistreated. He is angry!
He defends one of the Hebrews and kills an Egyptian. His anger – made him a murderer.

Moses runs for his life. Was this God's plan? _____.
God is not a murderer – Satan the devil is a murderer and has been from the beginning.

Moses' anger was used to get him out of God's plan for his life.

God always has a way of getting us back into His plan for our life even when we mess up and sin.

He comes to a well and meets the 7 daughters of the Priest of Midian. Moses is not afraid of anyone. He stands against the shepherds who harass the priest's daughters, then he proceeds to water their flocks.

Moses had courage and he was humble.

He lives there in Midian with the priest for 40 years. Moses is married and has sons; his life is in Midian – BUT GOD HAD A PLAN!

"FOR I KNOW THE THOUGHTS THAT I THINK TOWARD YOU, SAYS THE LORD, THOUGHTS OF PEACE AND NOT OF EVIL, TO GIVE YOU A FUTURE AND A HOPE."
JEREMIAH 29:11

WAYS TO GET OFF OF GOD's PLAN
Anger, Lying, Hating others
Stealing, disobeying our parents
The devil talks to our minds with lies and then our thoughts and emotions begin to agree with the devil
When we act on those thoughts and emotions
We get off the
Plan of God for our lives.

GOD'S PLAN

Ephesians 4:26 says,
"Be angry but sin not; let not the sun go down on your wrath"

Everyone gets angry but this verse is saying don't stay angry. Don't go to bed angry, your night prayer should be of one asking forgiveness and giving forgiveness.

Psalm 4:4 says,
Be angry and sin not."

Everyone gets angry but you don't have to sin.

Eccle. 7:9
"Do not hasten in your spirit to be angry."

Don't be a person who gets angry quickly.

1 John 4:20
"If someone says, "I love God," and hates his brother, he is a liar; for he who does not love his brother who he has seen how can he love God who he has not seen."

If you love God, you won't hate anyone!

"THESE SIX THINGS THE LORD HATES, YES SEVEN ARE AN ABOMINATION TO HIM."
PROVERBS 6:19

1	A PROUD LOOK
2	A LYING TONGUE
3	HANDS THAT SHED INNOCENT BLOOD
4	A HEART THAT DEVISES WICKED PLANS
5	FEET THAT ARE QUICK TO RUN TO EVIL
6	A FALSE WITNESS WHO SPEAKS LIES
7	ONE WHO CAUSES CONFLICT AMONG BRETHREN

GOD'S PLAN

When God says something, it WILL come to pass.

Pharoah could say NO all he wanted but God said okay you won't let My people go. Then I will show you how powerful I AM. You can sit there on your throne as if you are in control and have all this power,
But I will show you I AM THE ONE WITH POWER!

Can you cause the water to become blood?
Can you stop the frogs?
Can you stop the lice?
Can you stop the flies?
Can you stop your livestock from getting diseased?
Can you stop and be healed of boils?
Can you stop the locusts?
Can you stop the hail?
Can you make the Sunshine?
Can you protect anyone from death?
What is the answer to all these questions?

The plagues are fun to learn about, but it really is serious. We can bring so much heartache and punishment on our lives because we won't do what God says to do!
Pharoah brought this on his own land and his own people because he refused to honor God the Supreme Authority, Let's make sure all our lives we put God's Way First which is to follow JESUS!

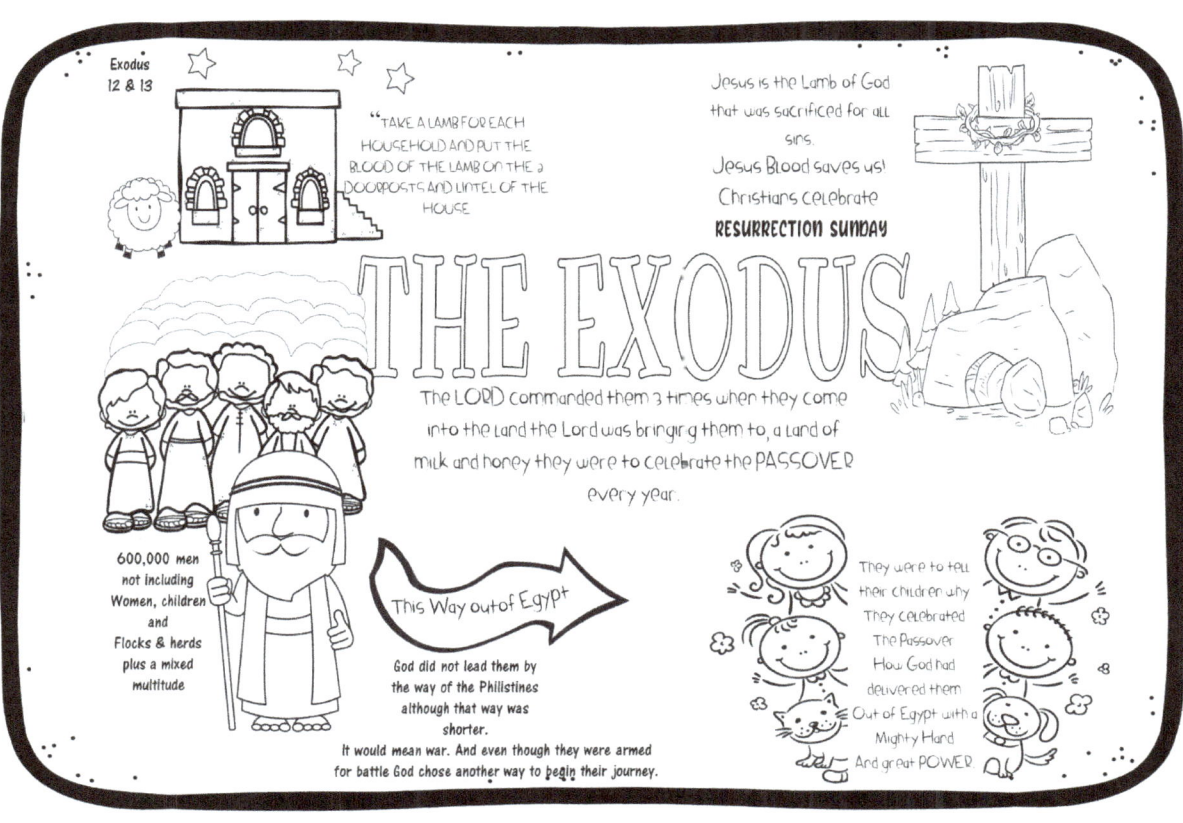

Exodus 12 & 13

"TAKE A LAMB FOR EACH HOUSEHOLD AND PUT THE BLOOD OF THE LAMB ON THE 2 DOORPOSTS AND LINTEL OF THE HOUSE"

Jesus is the Lamb of God that was sacrificed for all sins.
Jesus Blood saves us!
Christians celebrate
RESURRECTION SUNDAY

THE EXODUS

The LORD commanded them 3 times when they come into the land the Lord was bringing them to, a land of milk and honey they were to celebrate the PASSOVER every year.

600,000 men not including Women, children and Flocks & herds plus a mixed multitude

This Way out of Egypt

God did not lead them by the way of the Philistines although that way was shorter.
It would mean war. And even though they were armed for battle God chose another way to begin their journey.

They were to tell their children why They celebrated The Passover How God had delivered them Out of Egypt with a Mighty Hand And great POWER

LET MY people GO!

Color and then number each plague in the order they Came on the Egyptians

Which plague couldn't be copied by Pharaoh's magicians?

NO!

Pharaoh was prideful. He would not let God's people go and worship God. God sent plagues to show Pharaoh and all people there is no one greater than THE ONLY TRUE AND LIVING GOD!

#____

#____

#____

Memory Verse: Jeremiah 10:10
"But the LORD is the only true God.
He is the living God and the everlasting King!
The whole earth trembles at His anger. The nations cannot stand up to His wrath.

Let your LIGHT SHINE

Matthew 5:16

Sing to the LORD

Psalm 96

The LORD

gives wisdom
Proverbs 2:6

BE QUICK TO LISTEN

Be SLOW to speak or get angry. James 1:19

For God so loved the world, that he gave his only begotten Son,

that whosoever believeth in him should not perish, but have everlasting life.

John 3:16 KJV

GLORIOUS RESURRECTION!
Every day we celebrate
Jesus is alive!

THANK YOU

For downloading this April Resurrection Resource. I pray you and your children will be blessed, encouraged and your faith to abound.

As Christ followers we celebrate Resurrection Day. The world celebrates Easter. It is one day for the world. For us as Christ followers it is a daily celebration.

Easter comes early this year; the world will celebrate on April 4th and move on. Let's spend this whole month focusing on Jesus and the Journey to Resurrection!

Have a joyous Resurrection Day celebrating Jesus and our victory!

HOSANNA HOSANNA

But if the Spirit of Him that raised up Jesus from the dead dwell in you, He that raised Christ from the dead shall also quicken your mortal bodies by His Spirit that dwells in you.
Romans 8:11

Read
MARK 11:1-11

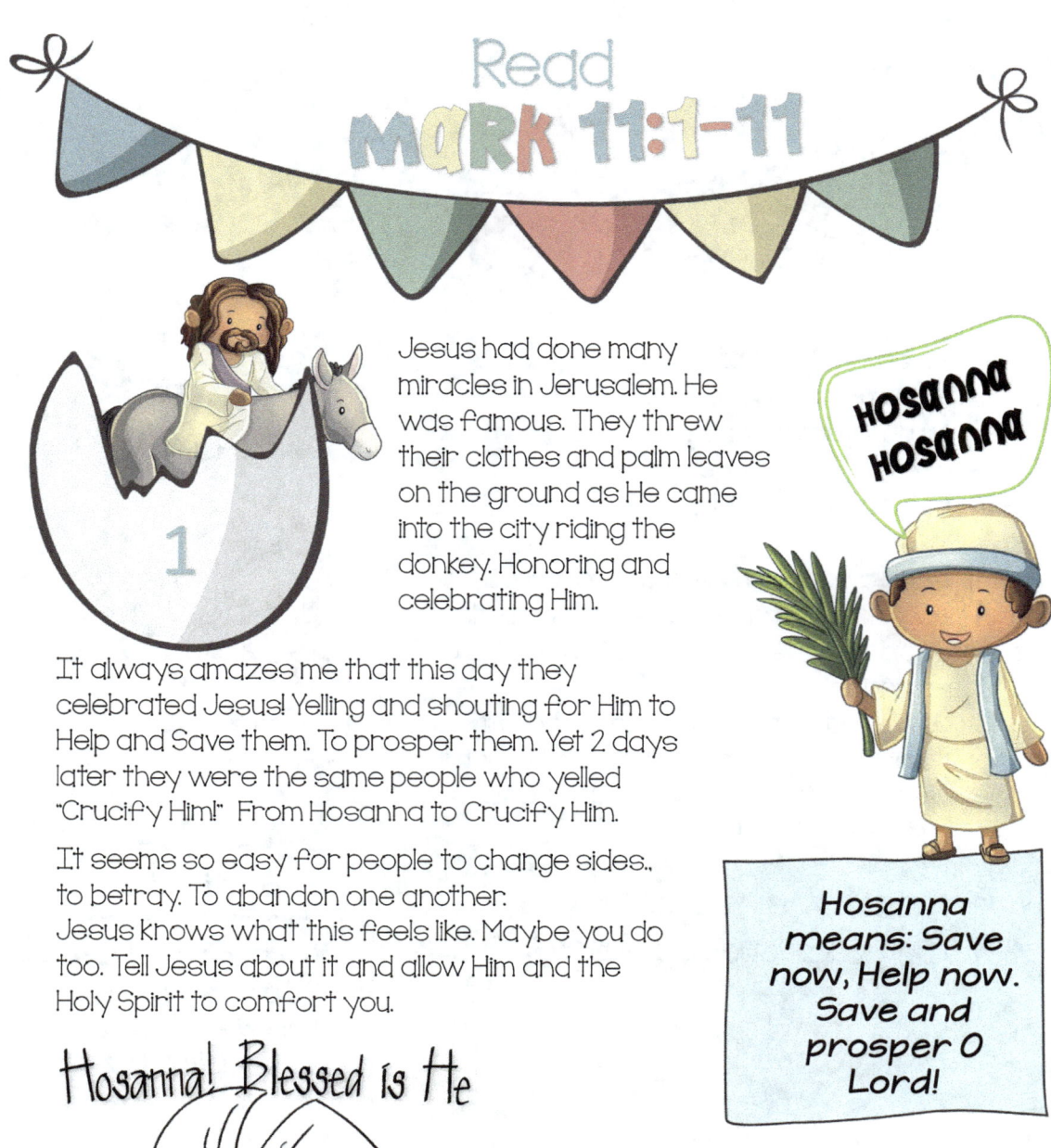

Jesus had done many miracles in Jerusalem. He was famous. They threw their clothes and palm leaves on the ground as He came into the city riding the donkey. Honoring and celebrating Him.

It always amazes me that this day they celebrated Jesus! Yelling and shouting for Him to Help and Save them. To prosper them. Yet 2 days later they were the same people who yelled "Crucify Him!" From Hosanna to Crucify Him.

It seems so easy for people to change sides.. to betray. To abandon one another. Jesus knows what this feels like. Maybe you do too. Tell Jesus about it and allow Him and the Holy Spirit to comfort you.

HOSanna
HOSanna

Hosanna means: Save now, Help now. Save and prosper O Lord!

Hosanna! Blessed is He

who comes in the name of the Lord!

And although God foretold all this would happen to Jesus. God's Word had to be fulfilled. Jesus said to Judas "The Word needs to be fulfilled but woe to whom the fulfillment comes."

Judas

Read
Mark 14:10-11
Matthew 26:14-16
Luke 22:1-6
John 13:2

What happened with Judas? The Bible says the Devil put it in his heart to betray Jesus. The devil can't just put anything into your heart. The devil looks for an open door into your heart. He found one in Judas.

I wonder what the open door could have been? Could it have been greed? He oversaw the money they had. Could it have been jealousy? He never was asked to go with Jesus he wasn't one of the top 3 leaders of Jesus (Peter, James and John)

Was he a double agent all along? Did he follow Jesus to say he was a part of the famous man yet really hated him like the Pharisees and the High Priest?

The "Why" really doesn't matter. For money, popularity, or revenge Judas loved himself more than Jesus.

He believed a lie. It cost him his life. The price was eternity In hell. His name will forever be associated with betrayal and murder.

Judas was one of Jesus' disciples	Judas was in Charge of The money	Judas went to the religious leader who wanted to kill Jesus He asked, "What will you give me to bring you Jesus?"	30 pieces of silver they gave Judas to betray Jesus

Judas is someone we should never forget Because the devil uses the same tricks and schemes on us God's children He continues to try to get us to betray Jesus and follow his promises. Because Satan promises things too The difference is he is a liar! The Bible says there NO TRUTH IN HIM! The promises he gives bring DEATH!

Judas
Cover it Story Board

KEEP A GUARD OVER YOUR HEART

Judas agrees to the 30 pieces and promises to give them Jesus	Jesus knew at it was Judas. He told the 12 "One of you will betray me. He who dips his bread in the bowl at the same time I do."	Judas betrayed Jesus with a kiss in the garden.	Once the devil had used Judas to get him to do Satan's work, he left Judas alone. Judas realized what he had done. He gave back the 30 pieces of silver. And he hung himself.

Fold and Glue over correct square

Fold and Glue over correct square

Fold and Glue over correct square

Fold and Glue over correct square

Cut the pictures keeping the flap attached. Then glue picture flap down in order of story.

Fold and Glue over correct square

Fold and Glue over correct square

Fold and Glue over correct square

Fold and Glue over correct square

The First Communion

Read

Matthew 26:17-30
Mark 14:12-26
Luke 22:7-23
John 13:1-35
1 Corinthians 11:23-32

This is a lot of reading
Split it up into 5 days

Jesus said, "As often as you eat this bread and drink the cup, you proclaim the Lord's death until He comes."
I Cor. 11:26

Stop & Take Communion

...an use cookies and milk, a torn bread or a cracker and juice. It's not the elements that matter its how you take it. WORTHLY- meaning stop and check your heart, have you sinned? Did you obey your parents, did you use mean words, did you get angry or throw something. Bow your head and ask Jesus to forgive you, once you've done this then lift the cookie, cracker, bread and thank Jesus for taking all the punishment of sin to His body. Eat, but take it all at once, Jesus took all the suffering at once. Then next you lift your cup and thank Jesus for His blood. Jesus shedding His blood brought salvation which equals = forgiveness, health, peace, safety, protection, prosperity, everything God said He has given us. Once this is done just put on some praise and worship music and dance and lift your hands to the Lord, during the slow worship songs get on your knees and lift your hands. Then let the music stop and just sit quietly for a minute. Let Jesus touch you.

New Covenant

Jesus said the bread and cup, or Communion was now a new Covenant in His blood. God made a covenant with Abraham and now Jesus is saying there is a New Covenant by His Blood. Abraham although the Bible says he was so righteous because of His faith he had to continually sacrifice unblemished lambs to cover his sins. With Jesus dying on the cross for us, all sins are forgiven once and for all. We don't need to sacrifice lambs anymore to be forgiven. We just need to receive His sacrifice. His blood to cover all our sins. We not only have His blood, but when we accept His sacrifice, we are born again, meaning our spirit becomes born and now we become a son or daughter of Almighty God just as much as Jesus is. If you haven't received Jesus' sacrifice you can do it now, just bow your head and pray this prayer:

Jesus, I am a sinner. There is nothing and no one who could have cleansed me from my sin. I believe You are the Son of God. I believe you came to earth as a baby and lived your life on earth without sinning. I believe you died for all sins including mine. I believe that in 3 days you rose from the grave defeating Satan. I believe that when I receive your sacrifice I am redeemed (meaning you paid the price to set me free from Satan's power), I receive your sacrifice and your victory. I am now born again. I am now God's child. Father God please fill me with your great Holy Spirit to help me live this life like Jesus did. In Jesus name I pray this Amen. WELCOME TO THE FAMILY! HALLELUJAH! Write this day down in your Bible, it's your "New Birth-Day!"

On the next pages fill in the secret verse.

Instructions: There is a picture above every blank square, write the FIRST letter the picture starts with: example:

Fill in all the empty squares with the first letter of each picture. Have fun!

Sun starts with S

Put the S in square

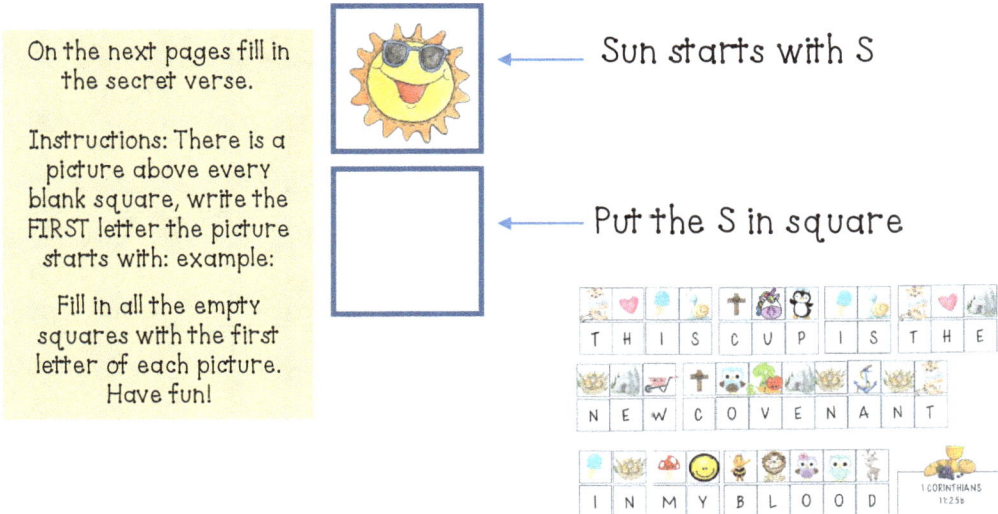

THIS CUP IS THE

NEW COVENANT

IN MY BLOOD

1 CORINTHIANS 11:25b

Jesus said

1 CORINTHIANS
11:25b

PETER, PETER, PETER

Read
Matthew 26:31-35
Mark 14:27-31
Luke 22:31-34
John 13:36-38

Peter was a disciple of Jesus. There are many who criticize Peter, but I see him as one that even though his faith wavered, he had faith. I see a man that truly believed he would die for Christ, but he didn't have the power or faith to see it through. He still loved his life more than Jesus. I see a man who had a greater fear of people than a Fear of God. I see how it's easy to say one thing and do another.

Aren't we like that also. We say we are going to obey our parents, we ask Jesus for forgiveness when we say things, we shouldn't but then we do what we said we wouldn't do again.

Peter wasn't supposed to deny Jesus. Jesus warned him:

1. Jesus said, "Pray that you fall not into temptation.
2. Peter "Satan has asked to sift you" but when you return strengthen your brothers.
3. Peter, before the rooster crows you will deny me 3 times.

> "Peter, before The rooster crows you will have denied Me 3 times."

Peter didn't obey. He didn't listen to the warnings. He may have heard them but he thought he was strong in himself. If he would have listened and followed Jesus' warning and instructions. But Jesus knew he wouldn't so Jesus could say, "Before the rooster crows you will deny Me 3 times."

Your parents tell you don't do that because this will happen. How often do you hear but you don't do what they say, because the temptation or what you want is more important than obeying?

PETER, PETER, PETER

Read
Matthew 26:31-35
Mark 14:27-31
Luke 22:31-34
John 13:36-38

Sift: To agitate and prove by trials and afflictions or troubles.

Jesus tells Peter, "Satan has asked to sift you." He didn't even ask what does that mean? What should I do?

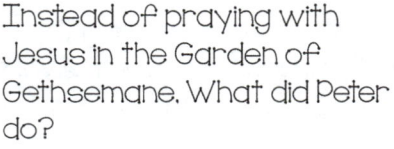

Instead of praying with Jesus in the Garden of Gethsemane. What did Peter do?

How many times did someone say to Peter that night while Jesus was before Pilot "You were with Jesus of Nazareth."
Each time he denied Jesus. The last time when he denied, the rooster crowed, and Peter remembered what Jesus had told him. Peter cried and runs away. He knows what he has done.
Denied Jesus _____ times.

Cut out the pictures below and glue them in the correct square

CROWN OF THORNS

Read
Matthew 27:27-31
Mark 15:16-201
Luke 22:63-65   John 19:1-16

Satan always mocks God. Satan thinks he's won. How silly of him to think he could out win God Almighty. The God Who created him. Satan always is looking for someone to do his dirty work. He uses anyone who is full of themselves. In my day they would say conceited. Meaning you think so highly of your self: you think you are the best, the cutest, the greatest. This thinking is what got Satan thrown out of heaven.

These soldiers mocked Jesus. They thought they were stronger and had Jesus conquered. They were doing the devil's work. But God had said this would be done way back in Genesis. In the garden of Eden.

God said to the Serpent, "He shall bruise your head, and you shall bruise his heel." Genesis 3:15b

That word "bruise" God tells the serpent in the garden who deceived Eve means to CRUSH. Think of this, to crush someone's head is a fatal blow it is a victory blow in a war you would be the Victor. To crush someone's heel means they may limp you hurt them, but it wasn't a victory blow.

Satan thought he had the victory by mocking Jesus. But he was just wounding his heel. The Victory was all God's.

THE NAILS 1 + 1 + 1

Have you ever had a splinter or pocked your finger or hand with a pin or something sharp? It hurts! Imagine those long thick nails and with a hammer they pounded those nails through Jesus' wrists all the way through and then into the wood of the cross. We can't even imagine how painful that would be.

They drove those nails not just in one hand/wrist but in both. Then they got his feet and pounded those nails into his feet all the way through to the wood.

It is gruesome! But sin is gruesome! I pray you never have to learn how gruesome, ugly, wicked and gross sin takes you too.

Jesus endured all this for you and for me. For the Whole world. Now you can understand why God Takes it seriously when we don't believe or trust Him with our lives.

He gave His only Son to go through all of this for Us.

The nails they say were 7-9 inches long They were more like spikes

Visual Action

1. Get a ruler use the ruler to draw a straight line and measure 9 inches below.
2. Make the line a nail/spike don't make it too think but don't make it too thin.
3. Measure your hand's thickness and mark how far the nail would have to go through to go through your hand... I'm sure there is a lot of nail left.

Visual Action below

THE CROSS
Read
Matthew 27:32-66
Mark 15:16-201
Luke 23:26-55   John 19:17-42
Isaiah 53

The Cross is what makes Christianity. What Jesus experienced and what the sacrifice the Cross bought for you and the whole world should be studied and put into our hearts. It is this Cross experience that changes lives.

So, for this part of the Journey to Resurrection let's take our time and really explore the Cross experience. As you read the different accounts as each Disciple writes about what they say, what they experienced, there are some variances. Why? Because each one of us has our own relationship with Jesus.

Christianity based on Jesus' crucifixion on the cross and His resurrection from the grave. This is not a religion. This is not just an experience. Jesus made the way for His Father to become our Father, so we could live in relationship with God.

Do you have many relatives? Do you have the same relationship with them all?. Do you have siblings, not all have the same relationship with your mom and dad even though their mon and/or day may be your mom and dad. Each one of us has been created different and as individuals. We each have our own relationship with Jesus and with God.

Just like the accounts of The Cross, many things happened that are the same, but what stood out to each one individual is what was written. What they remembered is slightly different. But it is all TRUTH. Truth is the main thing! God's Word is the only TRUTH. Each one told their account it also was told and written inspired by the HOLY SPIRIT – which is God's Spirit. Each story written, is how God showed each one of the Disciples the accounts though similar yet different. Each difference provides for us an additional piece to The Cross Experience.

> **On the next page is a template To make The Cross basket
> It will be filled as you cut the Eggs, color, and glue a sticker in each egg.
> Use this as a witnessing tool to friends and family. This will also put the
> Cross into your heart.**

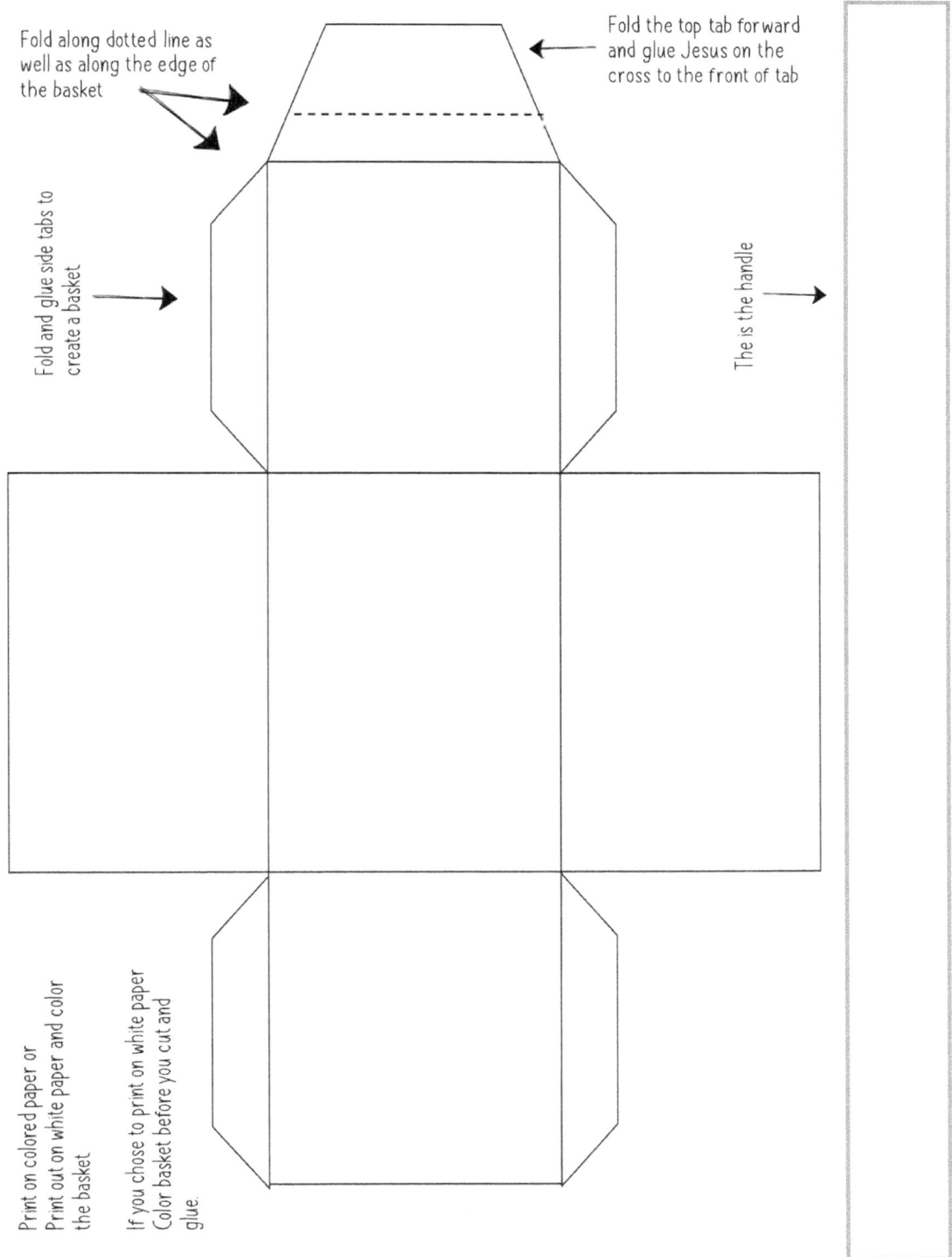

Fold along dotted line as well as along the edge of the basket

Fold the top tab forward and glue Jesus on the cross to the front of tab

Fold and glue side tabs to create a basket

The is the handle

Print on colored paper or Print out on white paper and color the basket

If you chose to print on white paper Color basket before you cut and glue.

There are 12 eggs to color or 12 colored eggs. Have fun you can color some or not color any.

You will need to cut out 12 eggs either colored eggs or those you are going to color. Do not cut them apart stop

When you cut eggs do not cut apart you want them to stay together so you can fold eggs like a book

Cut out and glue to front flap of basket keep cut the gray outside only.

Here is a finished Jesus basket With the eggs and the pictures glued inside each egg.

Cut out each picture and glue into the inside of an egg. Each pictures tells a portion of The Experience of the Cross

A certain man names Simon was told to carry the Cross for Jesus

How many robbers who were crucified with Jesus went to heaven That day?

They divided his clothes And cast lots

The purpose of the cross was to forgive sins once and for all

The accusation against Him was: King of the Jews

Jesus took His last breath. There was an earthquake, the rocks split, and the veil was torn from top to bottom

How many robbers Where crucified with him?

The Centurion when he saw all this said, Truly, this was the Son of God!

From the 6th hour to the 9th hour there was what?

The place they called where Jesus was crucified was called The Place of the Skull. Luke called it what? CALVARY

Jesus cried out? My God! My God! Why have You forsaken Me?

Joseph of Amalthea who was prominent council member took courage and asked Pilot for the body of Jesus and put it into the tomb and rolled the stone over it.

THE CROSS

Read

Genesis 3:15
John 3: 16
Colossians 2:15

There are 3 verses you need to put into your heart and in your mouth especially when the enemy tries to harm you with anything that is against God's will for your life. Use the next 2 pages to look up these verses and write them down. Then put them up and say them every day and every night. This will put them in your heart and then they will come out of your mouth especially when an attack from the enemy comes.

God Told The End From The Beginning

Nothing Ever surprises God!

Genesis 3:15

THE CROSS

John 3:16

No one could save us no one else could make the way to God and His eternal forgiveness
BUT JESUS COULD

THE CROSS

Colossians 2:15

Our fight now is a "good fight of FAITH!"

Jesus provided us

S — Saved us by eternally defeating Satan Colossians 2:15

A — Authority over Satan in Jesus Name Luke 10:19

L — God's love was poured into our hearts and His love never fails

V — Victory in every area if we believe and don't give up or quit

A — All things that pertain to life and Godliness.

T — Testimony when we don't quit and win battles in Jesus' name

I — In all these things we are MORE THAN Conquerors

O — Overcome this world by Our Faith

N — Name that is above all names – Jesus! His name is above anything and everything. Just say the name.

Below is a fun craft to color, cut, and glue.

Please color door and Jesus before cutting door out.
Cut door out and also cut along dotted line

I Am The Way The Truth The Life.

Color words
and graphics
Before
cutting out

Cut all
panels along
with the flap
leaving all
attached.

Leave attached
This will be the first panel glued to the back of door

Saved

Smash

ETERNALLY
DEFEATED
SATAN
Colossians
2:15

Authority

"Listen, I give
you the
authority to
trample on
serpents and
scorpions, and
over ALL the
power of the
enemy and
nothing shall by
any means hurt
you."
Luke 10:19

Love

In this the LOVE
of GOD was
manifested
toward us, that
God has sent His
only Begotten
Son into the
world, that we
might live
through HIM.
1 John 4:9

Victory

FAITH

HIS BLOOD GAVE US ETERNAL
LIFE
JUSTIFIED US
SET US APART
VICTORY OVER SIN AND THE
DEVIL

Color words
and graphics
Before
cutting out

Cut all
panels along
with the flap
leaving all
attached.

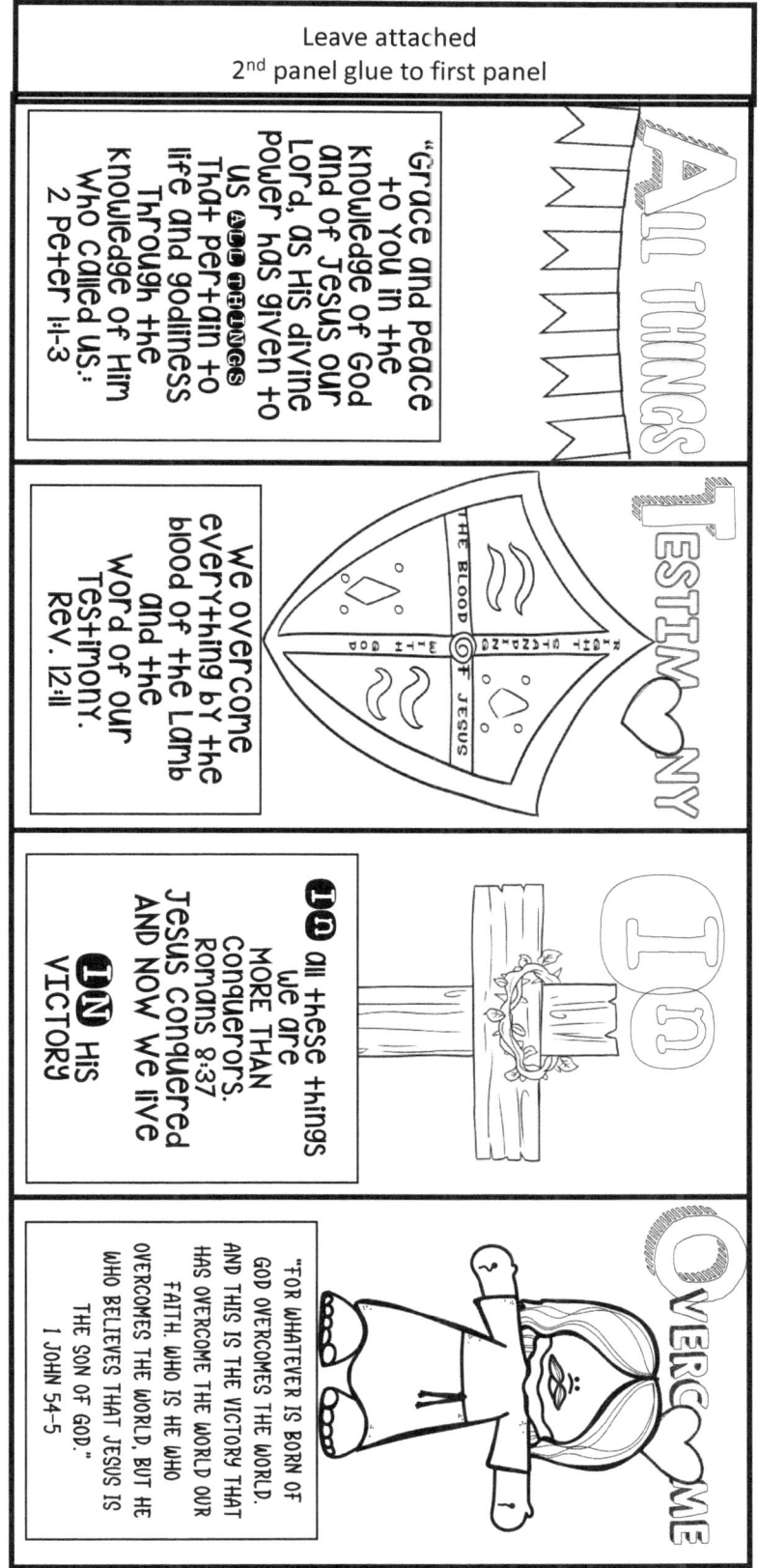

Leave attached
2nd panel glue to first panel

Line up and
attach here

All Things

"Grace and peace to you in the knowledge of God and of Jesus our Lord, as His divine power has given to us all things that pertain to life and godliness Through the knowledge of Him who called us.:
2 Peter 1:1-3

Testimony

We overcome everything by the blood of the Lamb and the word of our Testimony.
Rev. 12:11

THE BLOOD OF JESUS
RIGHT OFFERED WITH GOD

In

In all these things we are MORE THAN conquerors.
Romans 8:37
Jesus Conquered AND NOW we live IN HIS VICTORY

Overcome

"FOR WHATEVER IS BORN OF GOD OVERCOMES THE WORLD, AND THIS IS THE VICTORY THAT HAS OVERCOME THE WORLD OUR FAITH. WHO IS HE WHO OVERCOMES THE WORLD, BUT HE WHO BELIEVES THAT JESUS IS THE SON OF GOD."
1 JOHN 54-5

Glue 2ⁿᵈ panel to 3ʳᵈ panel here

Line up and
attach here

Color words
and graphics
Before
cutting out

This is one
Big panel
The dotted
line
Is to be
folded once
All panels
are attached.

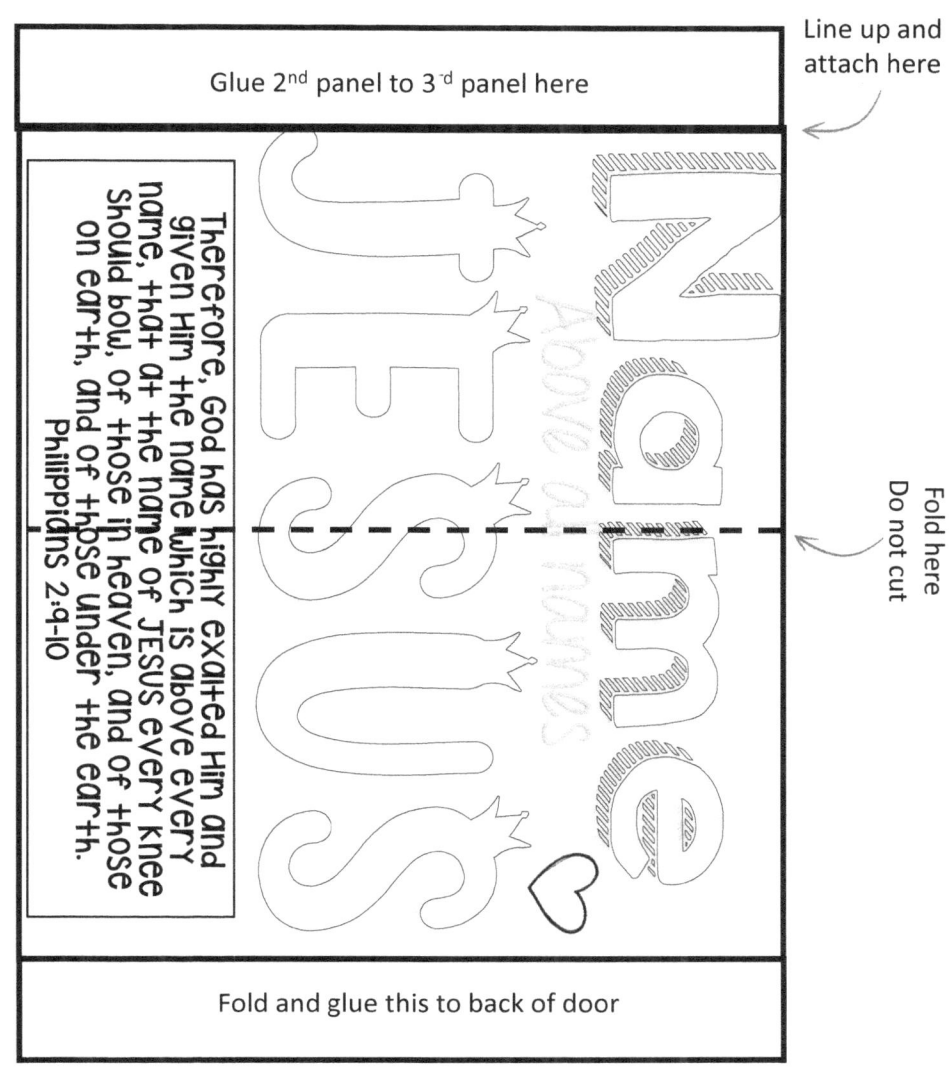

Name
above all names

JESUS

Therefore, God has highly exalted Him and
given Him the name which is above every
name, that at the name of JESUS every knee
should bow, of those in heaven, and of those
on earth, and of those under the earth.
Philippians 2:9-10

Fold here
Do not cut

Fold and glue this to back of door

Finishing instructions:
1. All panels will need to be accordion folded.
2. To attach to doors make sure doors are lined up then attach panel #1 to left side, and panel #3 to right side of doors.
3. Then children can open the doors and all the panels will be displayed like a book.

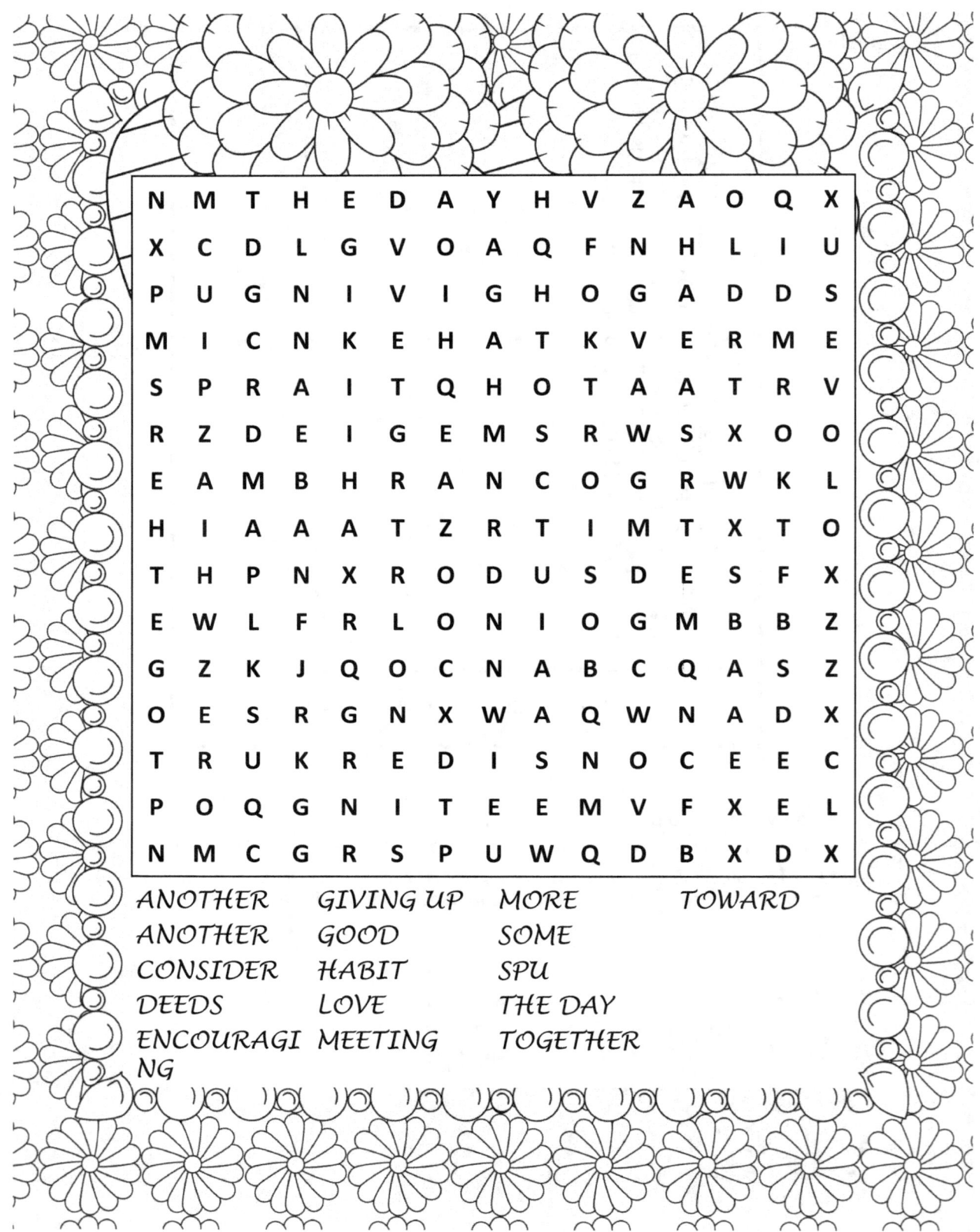

```
N M T H E D A Y H V Z A O Q X
X C D L G V O A Q F N H L I U
P U G N I V I G H O G A D D S
M I C N K E H A T K V E R M E
S P R A I T Q H O T A A T R V
R Z D E I G E M S R W S X O O
E A M B H R A N C O G R W K L
H I A A T Z R T I M T X T O
T H P N X R O D U S D E S F X
E W L F R L O N I O G M B B Z
G Z K J Q O C N A B C Q A S Z
O E S R G N X W A Q W N A D X
T R U K R E D I S N O C E E C
P O Q G N I T E E M V F X E L
N M C G R S P U W Q D B X D X
```

ANOTHER	GIVING UP	MORE	TOWARD
ANOTHER	GOOD	SOME	
CONSIDER	HABIT	SPU	
DEEDS	LOVE	THE DAY	
ENCOURAGI NG	MEETING	TOGETHER	

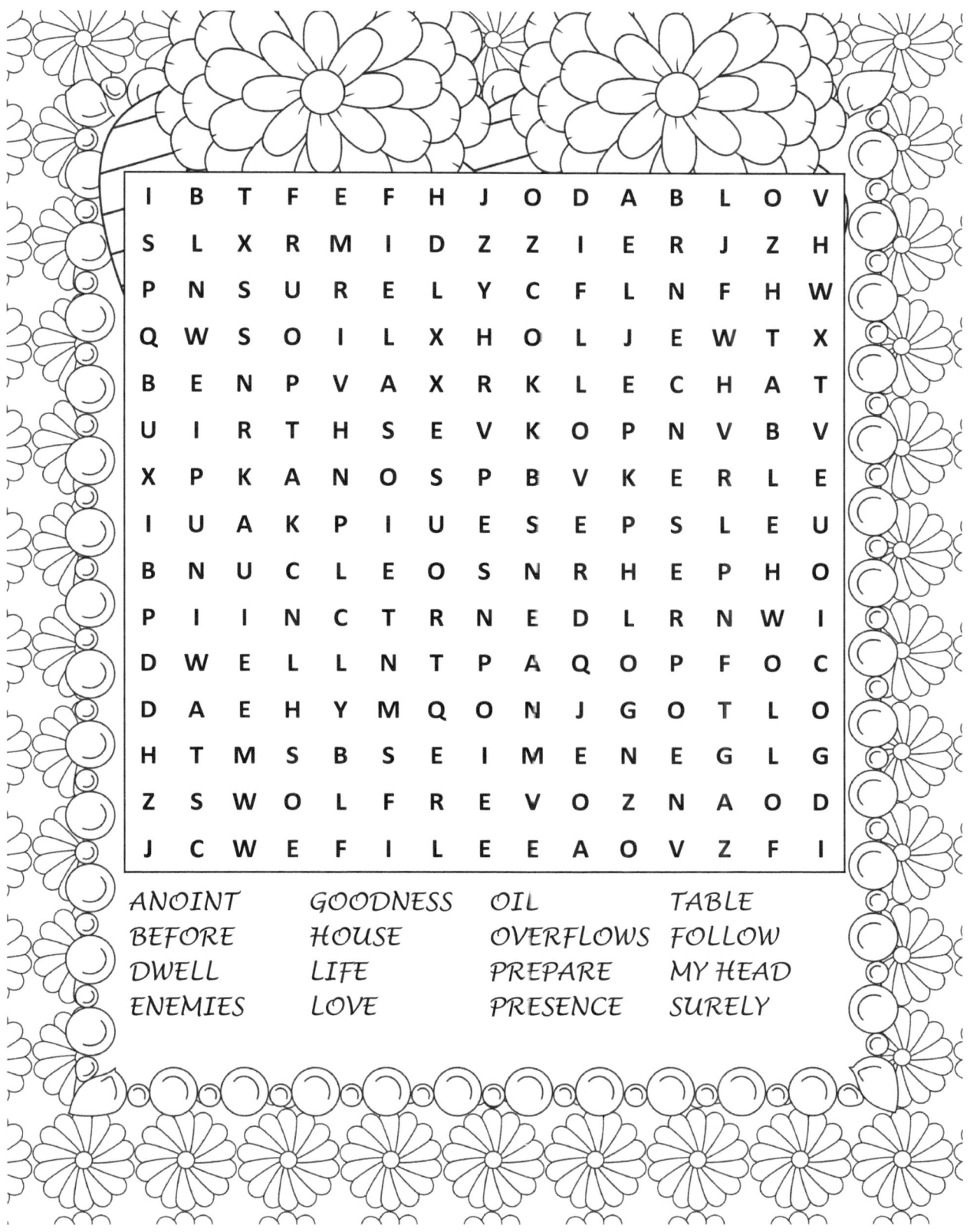

I	B	T	F	E	F	H	J	O	D	A	B	L	O	V
S	L	X	R	M	I	D	Z	Z	I	E	R	J	Z	H
P	N	S	U	R	E	L	Y	C	F	L	N	F	H	W
Q	W	S	O	I	L	X	H	O	L	J	E	W	T	X
B	E	N	P	V	A	X	R	K	L	E	C	H	A	T
U	I	R	T	H	S	E	V	K	O	P	N	V	B	V
X	P	K	A	N	O	S	P	B	V	K	E	R	L	E
I	U	A	K	P	I	U	E	S	E	P	S	L	E	U
B	N	U	C	L	E	O	S	N	R	H	E	P	H	O
P	I	I	N	C	T	R	N	E	D	L	R	N	W	I
D	W	E	L	L	N	T	P	A	Q	O	P	F	O	C
D	A	E	H	Y	M	Q	O	N	J	G	O	T	L	O
H	T	M	S	B	S	E	I	M	E	N	E	G	L	G
Z	S	W	O	L	F	R	E	V	O	Z	N	A	O	D
J	C	W	E	F	I	L	E	E	A	O	V	Z	F	I

ANOINT	GOODNESS	OIL	TABLE
BEFORE	HOUSE	OVERFLOWS	FOLLOW
DWELL	LIFE	PREPARE	MY HEAD
ENEMIES	LOVE	PRESENCE	SURELY

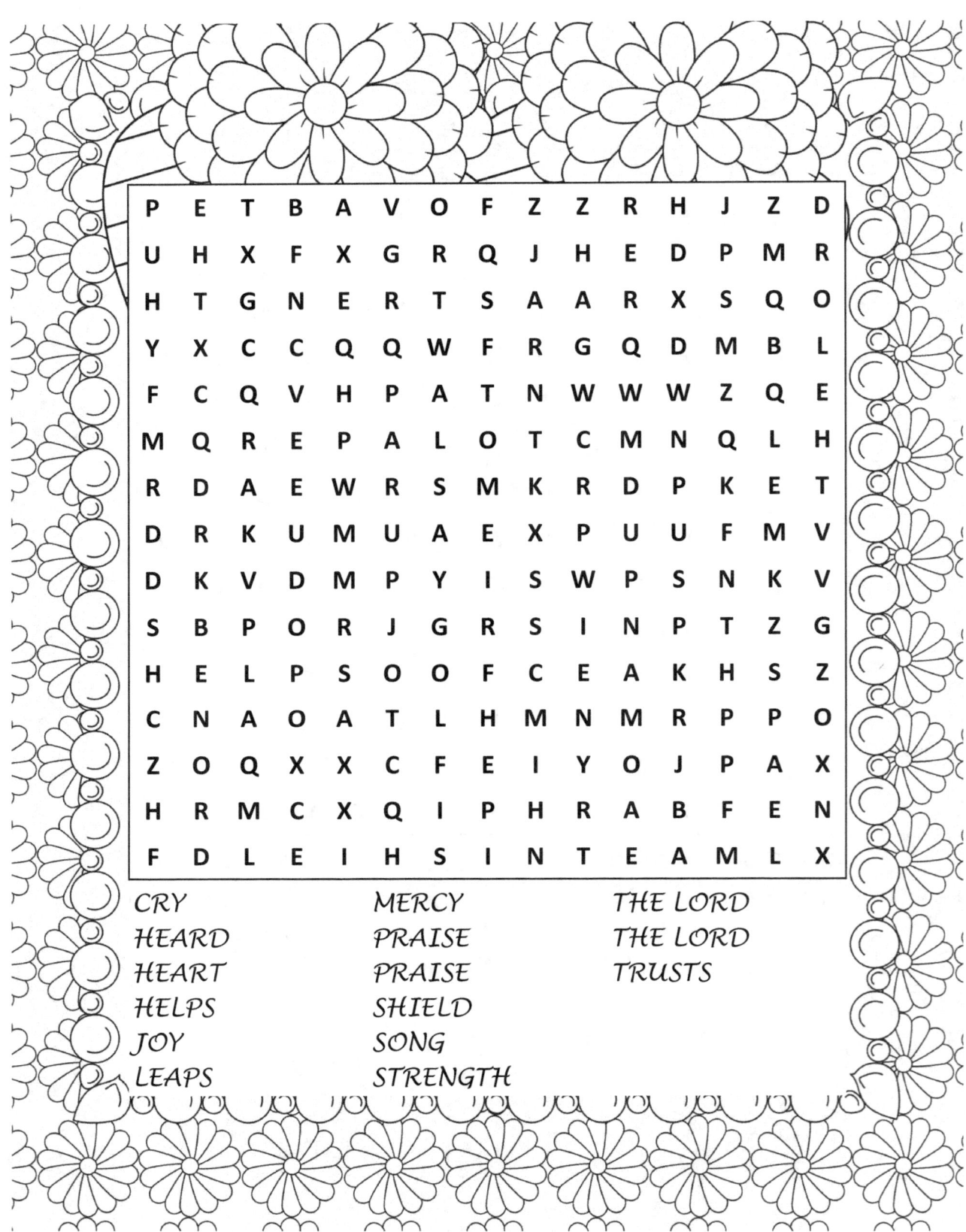

```
P  E  T  B  A  V  O  F  Z  Z  R  H  J  Z  D
U  H  X  F  X  G  R  Q  J  H  E  D  P  M  R
H  T  G  N  E  R  T  S  A  A  R  X  S  Q  O
Y  X  C  C  Q  Q  W  F  R  G  Q  D  M  B  L
F  C  Q  V  H  P  A  T  N  W  W  W  Z  Q  E
M  Q  R  E  P  A  L  O  T  C  M  N  Q  L  H
R  D  A  E  W  R  S  M  K  R  D  P  K  E  T
D  R  K  U  M  U  A  E  X  P  U  U  F  M  V
D  K  V  D  M  P  Y  I  S  W  P  S  N  K  V
S  B  P  O  R  J  G  R  S  I  N  P  T  Z  G
H  E  L  P  S  O  O  F  C  E  A  K  H  S  Z
C  N  A  O  A  T  L  H  M  N  M  R  P  P  O
Z  O  Q  X  X  C  F  E  I  Y  O  J  P  A  X
H  R  M  C  X  Q  I  P  H  R  A  B  F  E  N
F  D  L  E  I  H  S  I  N  T  E  A  M  L  X
```

CRY	*MERCY*	*THE LORD*
HEARD	*PRAISE*	*THE LORD*
HEART	*PRAISE*	*TRUSTS*
HELPS	*SHIELD*	
JOY	*SONG*	
LEAPS	*STRENGTH*	

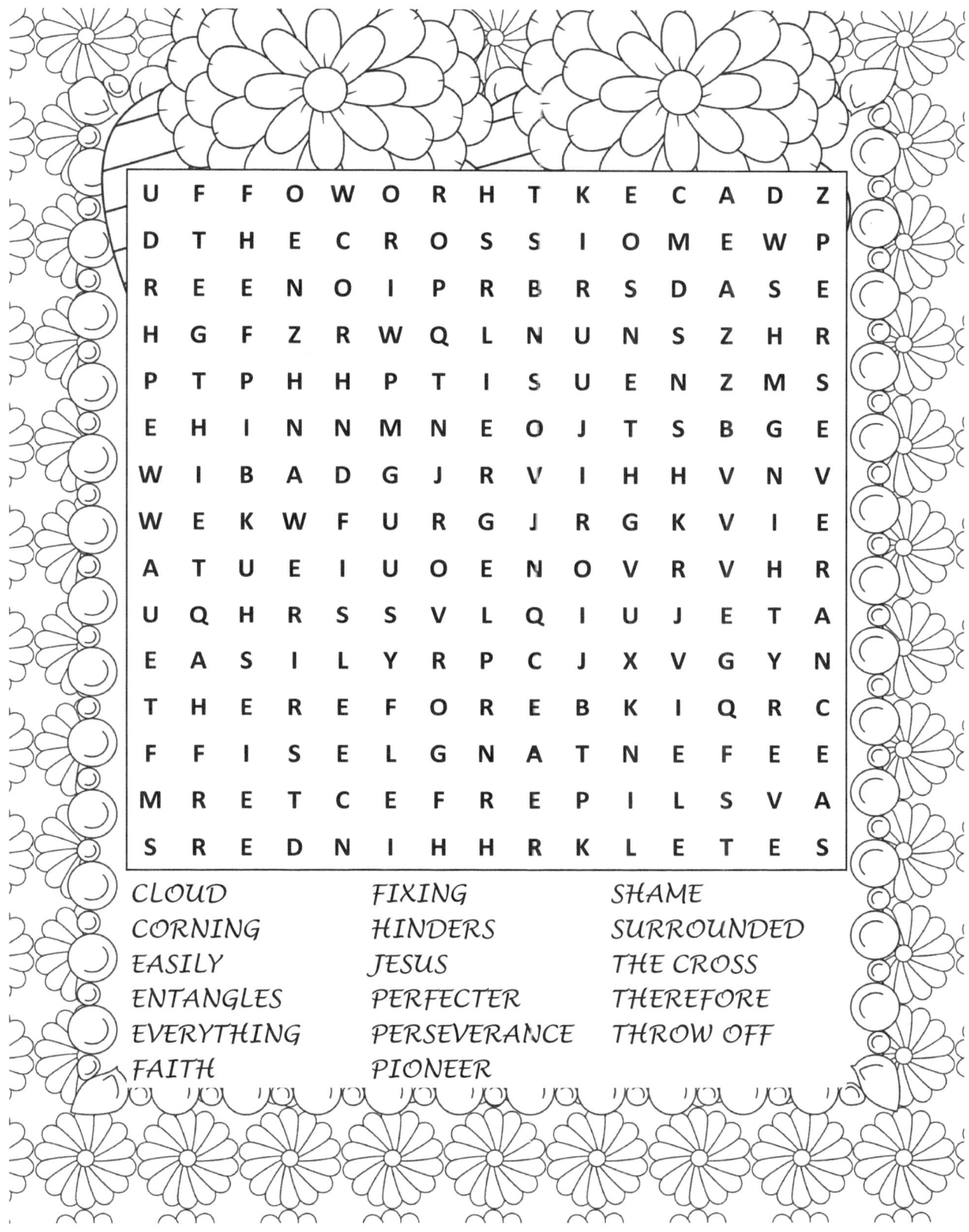

```
U F F O W O R H T K E C A D Z
D T H E C R O S S I O M E W P
R E E N O I P R B R S D A S E
H G F Z R W Q L N U N S Z H R
P T P H H P T I S U E N Z M S
E H I N M N E O J T S B G E
W I B A D G J R V I H H V N V
W E K W F U R G J R G K V I E
A T U E I U O E N O V R V H R
U Q H R S S V L Q I U J E T A
E A S I L Y R P C J X V G Y N
T H E R E F O R E B K I Q R C
F F I S E L G N A T N E F E E
M R E T C E F R E P I L S V A
S R E D N I H H R K L E T E S
```

CLOUD   FIXING   SHAME
CORNING   HINDERS   SURROUNDED
EASILY   JESUS   THE CROSS
ENTANGLES   PERFECTER   THEREFORE
EVERYTHING   PERSEVERANCE   THROW OFF
FAITH   PIONEER

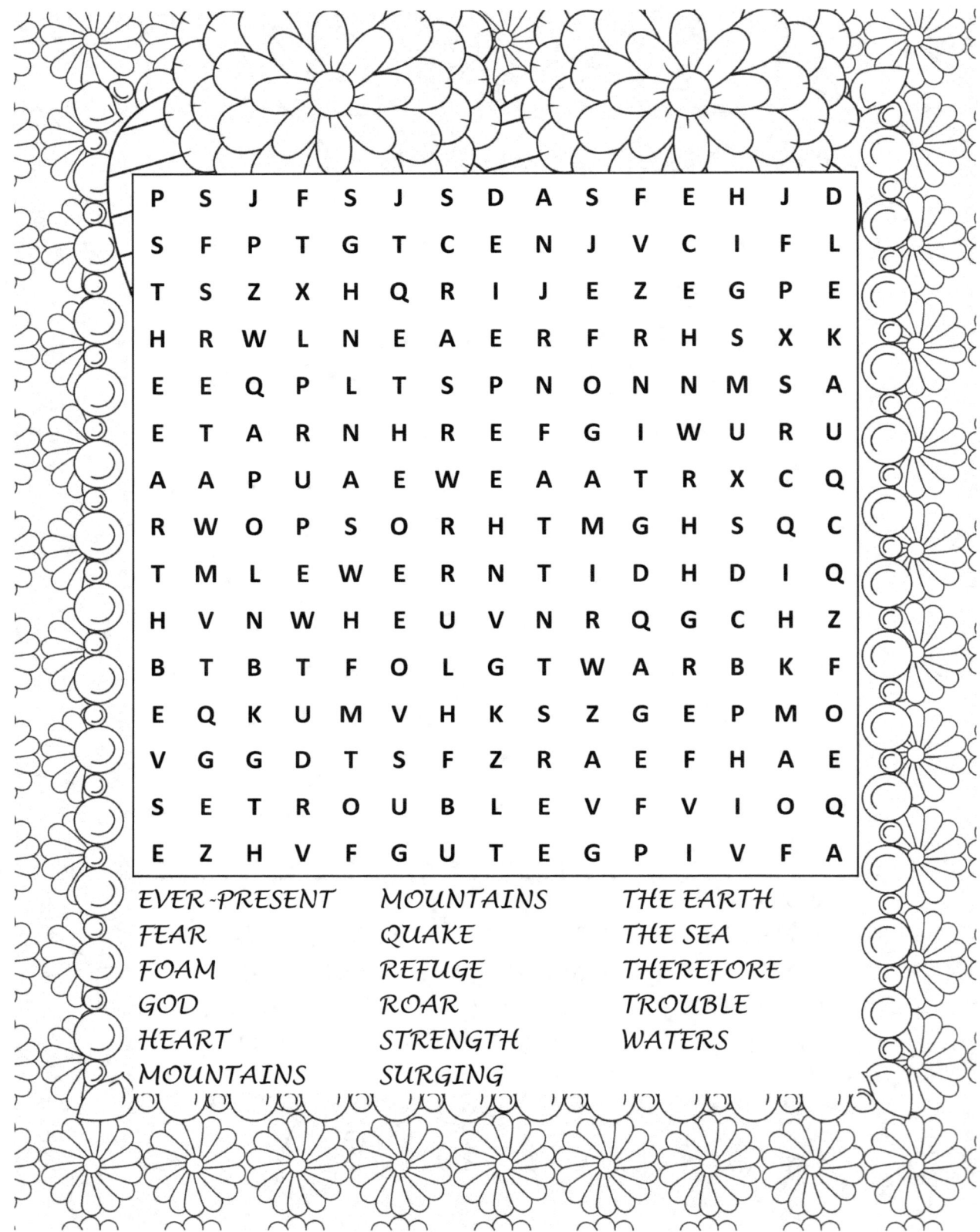

P	S	J	F	S	J	S	D	A	S	F	E	H	J	D
S	F	P	T	G	T	C	E	N	J	V	C	I	F	L
T	S	Z	X	H	Q	R	I	J	E	Z	E	G	P	E
H	R	W	L	N	E	A	E	R	F	R	H	S	X	K
E	E	Q	P	L	T	S	P	N	O	N	N	M	S	A
E	T	A	R	N	H	R	E	F	G	I	W	U	R	U
A	A	P	U	A	E	W	E	A	A	T	R	X	C	Q
R	W	O	P	S	O	R	H	T	M	G	H	S	Q	C
T	M	L	E	W	E	R	N	T	I	D	H	D	I	Q
H	V	N	W	H	E	U	V	N	R	Q	G	C	H	Z
B	T	B	T	F	O	L	G	T	W	A	R	B	K	F
E	Q	K	U	M	V	H	K	S	Z	G	E	P	M	O
V	G	G	D	T	S	F	Z	R	A	E	F	H	A	E
S	E	T	R	O	U	B	L	E	V	F	V	I	O	Q
E	Z	H	V	F	G	U	T	E	G	P	I	V	F	A

EVER-PRESENT	*MOUNTAINS*	*THE EARTH*
FEAR	*QUAKE*	*THE SEA*
FOAM	*REFUGE*	*THEREFORE*
GOD	*ROAR*	*TROUBLE*
HEART	*STRENGTH*	*WATERS*
MOUNTAINS	*SURGING*	

```
H  K  J  W  D  S  N  L  W  S  I  F  O  L  D
K  X  T  H  J  E  U  D  J  I  A  C  V  A  A
A  I  D  H  L  O  G  G  Q  I  N  R  L  G  V
O  A  Q  F  O  L  I  U  N  H  G  G  A  D  S
L  R  E  B  J  Z  G  T  Z  W  H  K  S  A  K
R  N  A  S  Z  H  P  I  K  A  Q  T  R  Z  D
M  R  S  O  E  U  T  N  L  L  I  O  R  V  Z
O  X  L  J  S  L  J  G  H  K  L  Z  I  C  M
E  E  G  U  Z  T  G  D  N  V  H  G  E  T  X
S  M  V  E  R  R  J  A  B  E  R  W  O  Q  E
G  R  O  W  G  V  B  H  E  B  R  O  E  W  O
E  Y  R  A  E  W  K  U  H  K  H  T  G  E  R
R  O  U  G  T  J  R  E  E  P  O  H  S  N  Q
T  U  F  V  J  G  O  I  U  W  S  N  B  E  R
D  R  O  L  E  H  T  J  K  M  N  J  X  R  K
```

EAGLES   STRENGTH
FAINT   THE LORD
GROW   WALK
HOPE   WEARY
RENEW   WINGS
SOAR

69

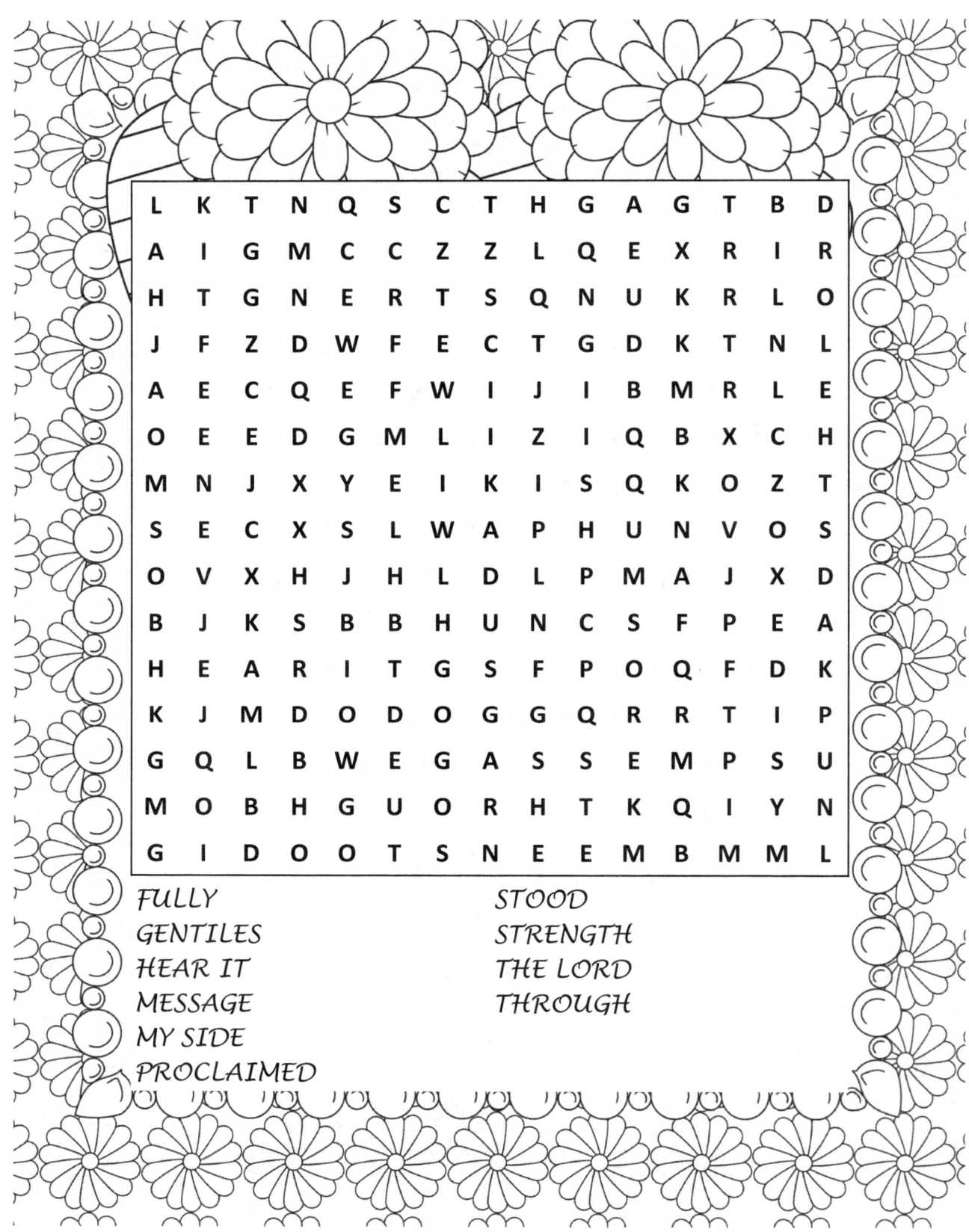

```
L K T N Q S C T H G A G T B D
A I G M C C Z Z L Q E X R I R
H T G N E R T S Q N U K R L O
J F Z D W F E C T G D K T N L
A E C Q E F W I J I B M R L E
O E E D G M L I Z I Q B X C H
M N J X Y E I K I S Q K O Z T
S E C X S L W A P H U N V O S
O V X H J H L D L P M A J X D
B J K S B B H U N C S F P E A
H E A R I T G S F P O Q F D K
K J M D O D O G G Q R R T I P
G Q L B W E G A S S E M P S U
M O B H G U O R H T K Q I Y N
G I D O O T S N E E M B M M L
```

FULLY   *STOOD*
GENTILES   *STRENGTH*
HEAR IT   *THE LORD*
MESSAGE   *THROUGH*
MY SIDE
PROCLAIMED

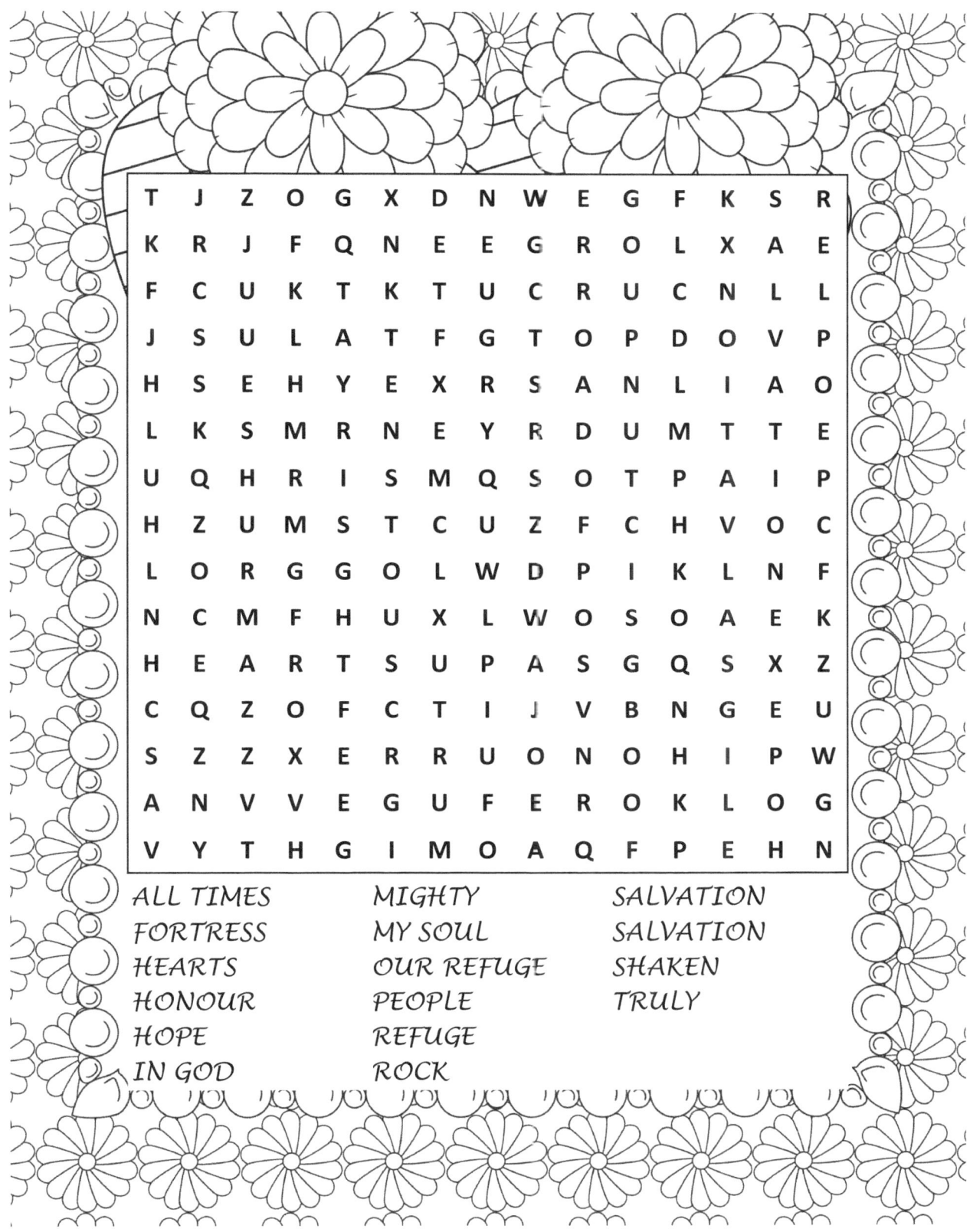

T	J	Z	O	G	X	D	N	W	E	G	F	K	S	R
K	R	J	F	Q	N	E	E	G	R	O	L	X	A	E
F	C	U	K	T	K	T	U	C	R	U	C	N	L	L
J	S	U	L	A	T	F	G	T	O	P	D	O	V	P
H	S	E	H	Y	E	X	R	S	A	N	L	I	A	O
L	K	S	M	R	N	E	Y	R	D	U	M	T	T	E
U	Q	H	R	I	S	M	Q	S	O	T	P	A	I	P
H	Z	U	M	S	T	C	U	Z	F	C	H	V	O	C
L	O	R	G	G	O	L	W	D	P	I	K	L	N	F
N	C	M	F	H	U	X	L	W	O	S	O	A	E	K
H	E	A	R	T	S	U	P	A	S	G	Q	S	X	Z
C	Q	Z	O	F	C	T	I	J	V	B	N	G	E	U
S	Z	Z	X	E	R	R	U	O	N	O	H	I	P	W
A	N	V	V	E	G	U	F	E	R	O	K	L	O	G
V	Y	T	H	G	I	M	O	A	Q	F	P	E	H	N

ALL TIMES	MIGHTY	SALVATION
FORTRESS	MY SOUL	SALVATION
HEARTS	OUR REFUGE	SHAKEN
HONOUR	PEOPLE	TRULY
HOPE	REFUGE	
IN GOD	ROCK	

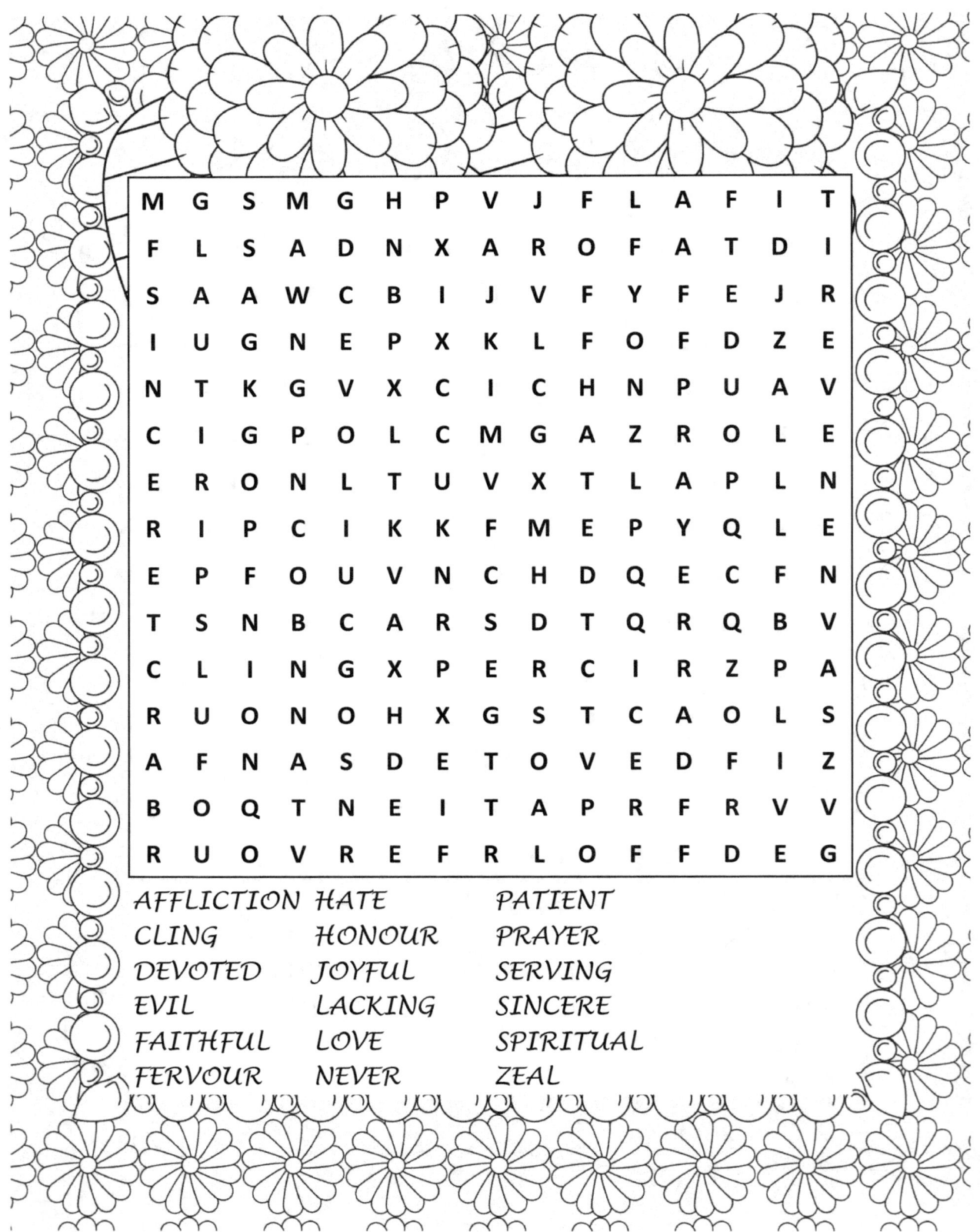

```
M G S M G H P V J F L A F I T
F L S A D N X A R O F A T D I
S A A W C B I J V F Y F E J R
I U G N E P X K L F O F D Z E
N T K G V X C I C H N P U A V
C I G P O L C M G A Z R O L E
E R O N L T U V X T L A P L N
R I P C I K K F M E P Y Q L E
E P F O U V N C H D Q E C F N
T S N B C A R S D T Q R Q B V
C L I N G X P E R C I R Z P A
R U O N O H X G S T C A O L S
A F N A S D E T O V E D F I Z
B O Q T N E I T A P R F R V V
R U O V R E F R L O F F D E G
```

AFFLICTION HATE   PATIENT
CLING   HONOUR   PRAYER
DEVOTED   JOYFUL   SERVING
EVIL   LACKING   SINCERE
FAITHFUL   LOVE   SPIRITUAL
FERVOUR   NEVER   ZEAL

```
E  I  X  H  Z  M  M  K  C  P  J  A  D  M  S
H  H  W  P  U  N  V  O  S  I  M  T  S  Q  B
Z  X  T  O  I  L  Q  U  D  W  B  H  E  K  S
U  G  B  G  G  D  V  O  E  K  W  C  S  S  U
Q  D  N  J  S  K  J  A  F  E  J  M  S  E  U
H  H  R  O  S  P  K  M  H  W  U  E  E  I  E
R  G  J  N  R  U  I  C  L  R  K  O  N  T  G
O  N  O  M  L  T  I  H  R  A  E  T  K  L  P
U  Q  W  S  O  E  S  K  S  P  O  Z  A  U  W
O  J  R  U  R  W  F  M  C  D  T  V  E  C  K
C  H  R  I  S  T  S  N  A  Q  R  V  W  I  P
C  J  J  H  T  D  H  L  O  G  I  A  H  F  K
L  G  V  O  A  T  H  G  I  L  E  D  H  F  K
P  E  R  S  E  C  U  T  I  O  N  S  O  I  U
S  T  L  U  S  N  I  M  O  Z  B  U  T  D  I
```

AM STRONG
AM WEAK
CHRIST'S
DELIGHT
DIFFICULTIES
HARDSHIPS

INSULTS
PERSECUTIONS
SAKE
WEAKNESSES

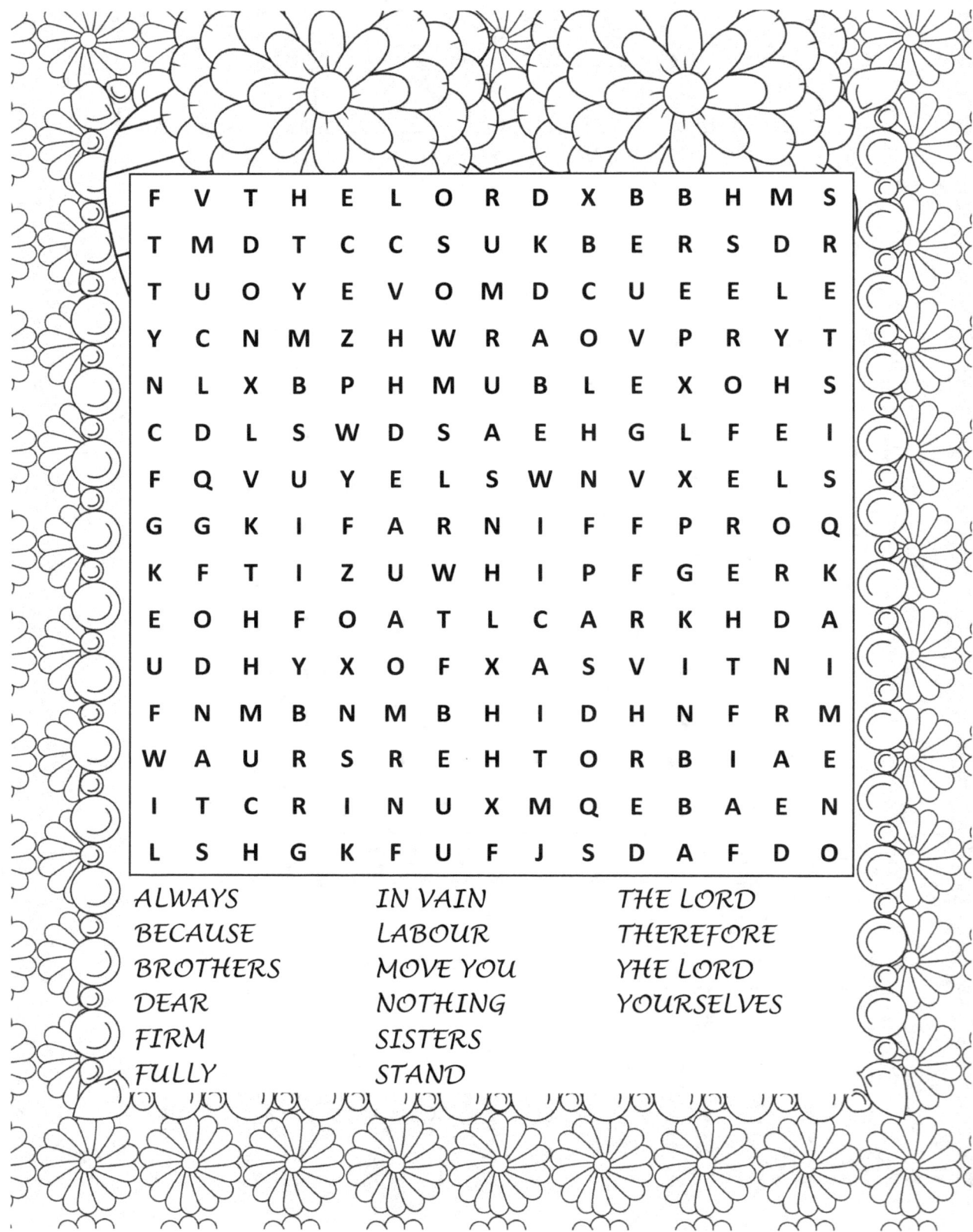

F	V	T	H	E	L	O	R	D	X	B	B	H	M	S
T	M	D	T	C	C	S	U	K	B	E	R	S	D	R
T	U	O	Y	E	V	O	M	D	C	U	E	E	L	E
Y	C	N	M	Z	H	W	R	A	O	V	P	R	Y	T
N	L	X	B	P	H	M	U	B	L	E	X	O	H	S
C	D	L	S	W	D	S	A	E	H	G	L	F	E	I
F	Q	V	U	Y	E	L	S	W	N	V	X	E	L	S
G	G	K	I	F	A	R	N	I	F	F	P	R	O	Q
K	F	T	I	Z	U	W	H	I	P	F	G	E	R	K
E	O	H	F	O	A	T	L	C	A	R	K	H	D	A
U	D	H	Y	X	O	F	X	A	S	V	I	T	N	I
F	N	M	B	N	M	B	H	I	D	H	N	F	R	M
W	A	U	R	S	R	E	H	T	O	R	B	I	A	E
I	T	C	R	I	N	U	X	M	Q	E	B	A	E	N
L	S	H	G	K	F	U	F	J	S	D	A	F	D	O

ALWAYS   IN VAIN   THE LORD
BECAUSE   LABOUR   THEREFORE
BROTHERS   MOVE YOU   YHE LORD
DEAR   NOTHING   YOURSELVES
FIRM   SISTERS
FULLY   STAND

```
L W T R O U B L E E V O B I O
I U W A U K A V O Z V A V F T
W K J T N A T P W E I S S O W
L C S X U R I Q R U K K L O C
B I J G H T K C Q Q N D R T U
U M N E T C O N U K Y L O C N
S M A U T M T S W O D N J N U
J R U J E E L M U H S F X D N
T L D Q L F V F L B B Z Q L B
P N W L W N Q A U Z P L W R T
P E A C E C Q O H N L S V O O
L M S G N I H T E S E H T W K
P M O H T U L U E K A T Z E M
S S R T L O D V I I H K L H B
Q A V M B C P X A D K W O T W
```

HAVE   THESE THINGS
HEART   TOLD YOU
OVERCOME   TROUBLE
PEACE   WORLD
TAKE
THE WORLD

P	K	J	P	H	Z	L	C	L	D	K	B	X	V	H
J	D	E	S	J	E	M	A	J	C	E	V	A	E	S
M	O	A	V	I	D	A	H	O	H	M	O	G	G	T
Y	G	G	Q	S	S	L	V	I	G	G	V	N	U	R
S	P	R	I	Z	E	T	N	E	A	E	I	Q	J	A
E	G	H	P	B	R	D	E	D	N	T	H	E	M	I
L	H	O	L	D	K	E	U	R	T	W	S	T	H	N
F	P	P	U	F	A	M	D	E	S	U	A	O	E	I
T	A	K	E	N	K	E	G	I	S	V	D	R	M	N
T	P	O	P	V	R	R	H	I	S	K	X	N	D	G
V	S	X	W	I	O	H	M	A	R	N	R	X	E	G
D	V	I	W	F	C	G	D	R	A	W	O	T	L	R
W	Q	D	R	S	R	E	H	T	O	R	B	C	L	X
Z	X	A	R	H	V	R	E	M	L	V	P	R	A	M
E	Z	L	K	U	C	X	E	W	Q	Z	U	V	C	V

AHEAD   FORGETTING PRIZE
BEHIND   GOD   SISTERS
BROTHERS HEAVENWARD STRAINING
CALLED ME HOLD   TAKEN
CHRIST   JESUS   THE GOAL
CONSIDER MYSELF   TOWARD

H	J	D	S	F	X	N	L	E	J	C	A	I	F	L
B	B	Z	Q	Z	G	P	W	L	W	P	N	Q	B	Q
G	N	I	S	A	E	L	P	P	P	L	W	T	C	L
G	N	I	W	E	N	E	R	R	A	O	E	D	D	F
N	T	R	A	N	S	F	O	R	M	E	D	N	S	T
Z	U	E	P	X	D	V	Q	S	Q	K	I	I	C	D
C	F	S	P	S	G	T	N	N	X	Z	E	M	C	R
A	V	M	B	C	E	P	C	X	A	D	K	R	W	U
W	P	U	F	D	V	L	K	E	T	M	P	U	D	O
G	M	K	T	S	B	N	B	I	F	T	R	O	O	Z
C	O	N	F	O	R	M	D	A	M	R	Z	Y	O	K
P	O	A	M	N	W	O	R	L	D	Z	E	G	G	J
N	H	A	B	B	X	A	J	S	D	O	G	P	S	M
N	R	E	T	T	A	P	E	H	T	R	F	H	I	H
R	S	V	Q	U	J	E	R	G	J	T	G	J	H	R

ABLE   PLEASING   HIS GOOD   WORLD

APPROV   RENEWING   PERFECT   YOUR MIND

CONFORM   THE

               PATTERN

GOD'S   TRANSFORM

               ED

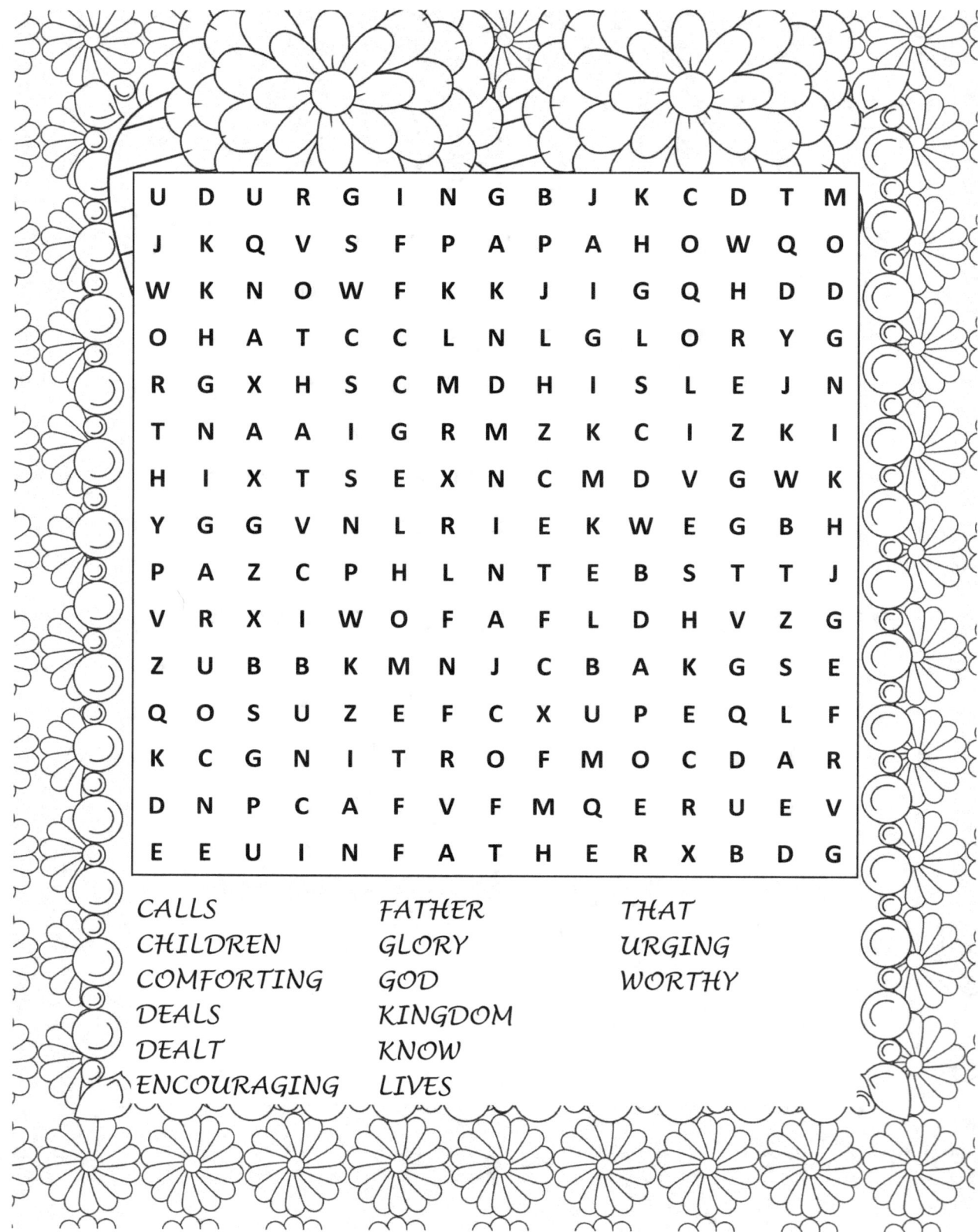

```
U D U R G I N G B J K C D T M
J K Q V S F P A P A H O W Q O
W K N O W F K K J I G Q H D D
O H A T C C L N L G L O R Y G
R G X H S C M D H I S L E J N
T N A A I G R M Z K C I Z K I
H I X T S E X C M D V G W K
Y G G V N L R I E K W E G B H
P A Z C P H L N T E B S T T J
V R X I W O F A L D H V Z G
Z U B B K M N J C B A K G S E
Q O S U Z E F C X U P E Q L F
K C G N I T R O F M O C D A R
D N P C A F V F M Q E R U E V
E E U I N F A T H E R X B D G
```

CALLS   FATHER   THAT
CHILDREN   GLORY   URGING
COMFORTING   GOD   WORTHY
DEALS   KINGDOM
DEALT   KNOW
ENCOURAGING   LIVES

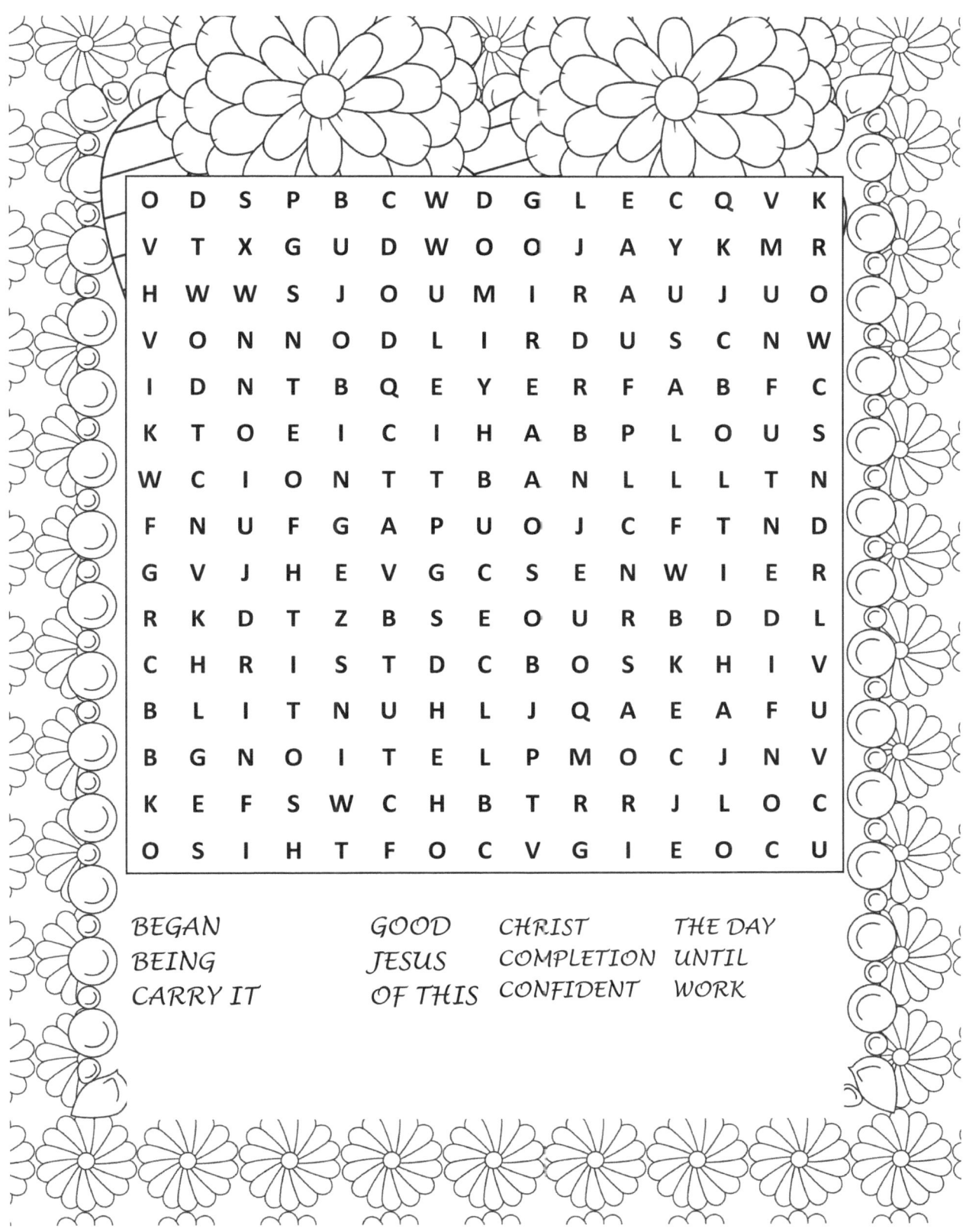

O	D	S	P	B	C	W	D	G	L	E	C	Q	V	K
V	T	X	G	U	D	W	O	O	J	A	Y	K	M	R
H	W	W	S	J	O	U	M	I	R	A	U	J	U	O
V	O	N	N	O	D	L	I	R	D	U	S	C	N	W
I	D	N	T	B	Q	E	Y	E	R	F	A	B	F	C
K	T	O	E	I	C	I	H	A	B	P	L	O	U	S
W	C	I	O	N	T	T	B	A	N	L	L	L	T	N
F	N	U	F	G	A	P	U	O	J	C	F	T	N	D
G	V	J	H	E	V	G	C	S	E	N	W	I	E	R
R	K	D	T	Z	B	S	E	O	U	R	B	D	D	L
C	H	R	I	S	T	D	C	B	O	S	K	H	I	V
B	L	I	T	N	U	H	L	J	Q	A	E	A	F	U
B	G	N	O	I	T	E	L	P	M	O	C	J	N	V
K	E	F	S	W	C	H	B	T	R	R	J	L	O	C
O	S	I	H	T	F	O	C	V	G	I	E	O	C	U

BEGAN	GOOD	CHRIST	THE DAY
BEING	JESUS	COMPLETION	UNTIL
CARRY IT	OF THIS	CONFIDENT	WORK

T	G	H	E	U	C	H	B	V	A	A	F	Z	I	F
J	N	U	H	H	R	T	M	H	W	A	H	B	E	R
H	J	A	M	P	W	V	L	S	L	G	C	C	L	Q
X	S	J	V	J	W	C	S	L	U	E	C	U	K	U
N	D	T	D	L	G	D	L	O	V	O	C	D	K	N
K	I	R	H	S	U	P	H	O	L	D	S	I	R	V
B	G	X	O	G	T	T	L	H	J	H	D	A	O	D
N	O	I	H	L	I	E	Z	A	V	F	W	K	J	I
L	X	R	M	V	E	L	P	S	Q	J	U	U	R	W
O	P	E	J	W	C	K	E	S	E	C	B	I	U	I
F	I	R	M	L	C	J	M	D	K	K	G	Q	R	O
U	F	T	J	R	E	P	S	U	D	I	A	R	D	H
H	H	K	B	E	B	L	E	D	N	A	H	M	R	S
I	O	B	E	Q	C	V	L	J	Z	G	U	A	O	C
E	L	B	M	U	T	S	J	X	X	P	H	X	L	G

DELIGHTS   LORD   UPHOLDS
FALL   MAKES
FIRM   STEPS
HAND   STUMBLE
LORD   THOUGH

TASK

Draw a face and then colour it

I'M WITH YOU!

I FOLD MY HANDS IN PRAYER

Remember

GOD'S Promises

Genesis 9:13-17

Check Out My Other Books

  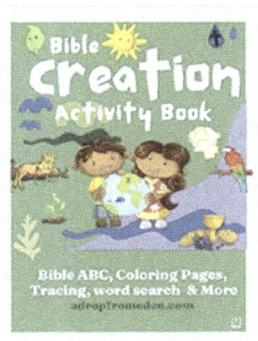